DRUGS: SUBSTANCE ABUSE

Second Edition

DRUGS: SUBSTANCE ABUSE

Second Edition

Kenneth L. Jones
Louis W. Shainberg
Curtis O. Byer

Mt. San Antonio College

CANFIELD PRESS
San Francisco
A Department of
Harper & Row, Publishers, Inc.

DRUGS: SUBSTANCE ABUSE, Second Edition

Library of Congress Cataloging in Publication Data

Jones, Kenneth Lamar, 1931-
    Drugs: substance abuse.

    First ed. published in 1970 under title: Drugs,
alcohol, and tobacco.
    Bibliography
    Includes index.
    1. Drug abuse.   2. Alcoholism.   3. Tobacco—
Physiological effect.   I. Shainberg, Louis W.,
joint author.   II. Byer, Curtis O., joint author.
III. Title.
RC566.J628   1975   362.2'9   75-1400

ISBN 0-06-384361-7

Cover and interior design by Penny L. Faron

PREFACE

Drugs of all kinds, including alcohol and tobacco, are very much a part of today's world. Not only do they strongly influence our personal health; they also directly affect our economy and the social, moral, and legal foundations of our society.

The use of drugs closely relates to our cultural concept of good health. That is, drugs are primarily used to treat diseases. Yet drugs can be, and are being, misused and abused to a point where they adversely affect health. Alcohol is used in a variety of social situations, yet its abuse can lead to alcoholism. The habitual use of tobacco is pleasurable for many people, yet the threat of cancer and heart disease from tobacco use has been well documented in recent years.

The purpose of health science is to draw those facts and principles from other scientific disciplines that relate directly to the solutions of present-day health problems. This book provides a basic body of knowledge for a contemporary understanding of the problems associated with the abuse of these substances.

In writing this new edition, we have attempted to reflect many of the changes that have occurred since the first edition in the legal status and medical evaluation of certain types of drugs. While new and improved treatment methods are being developed, the social pressures that have led to our nation's multifaceted drug problem remain.

Thus, the crucial factor is you, the individual. The validity of the decisions which you make about drug use must be based on accurate, up-to-date information. These decisions relate directly to your health, your personal happiness, and your community. We hope that this brief volume will contribute to the success of your personal choices.

16012

K.L.J.
C.O.B.
L.W.S.

CONTENTS

Chapter 1

SUBSTANCE USE AND ABUSE

If you were asked to define the word "drug," you might simply say that a drug is a substance used in treating a disease. However, a more complete definition would be: A drug is any substance, other than food, *that alters the body or its functions*.

The actions and effects of various drugs differ greatly. Some are so mild that their effects are almost imperceptible. Others are more powerful and can be dangerous if not taken exactly as prescribed. Still other drugs are not even recognized by the general public as drugs, although they are widely used in everyday life as well as in medicine and science. Caffeine, nicotine, and alcohol are used often, are socially acceptable by most, are legally marketed without medical advice, and are not generally considered drugs.

Drugs can be obtained by prescription or "over the counter." In general, drugs are not considered safe for the public to obtain without a prescription if they can create hazards for the person using them or for society. Drugs can be dangerous to society not as "good drugs," used medically or else socially acceptable although used nonmedically, but as "bad drugs," used not to improve physical health or reduce symptoms of illness, but as the *means* of *problem-solving behavior*. Some drugs play dual roles: For example, barbiturates and amphetamines are considered good drugs when used as sleeping pills, diet pills, or painkillers, but bad drugs when used as downers, uppers, or dope. Consequently, drug taking is a *behavior problem,* in which people overuse or abuse substances acceptable within their cultural or peer group to increase their pleasure, reduce discomfort, or obtain some other positive (for them) effect.

Medical Use of Drugs

The use of drugs dates back thousands of years. At first, drugs were used by primitive societies as part of their religious healing ceremonies; in most of these societies, however, more reliance was placed on prayers, incantations, and charms than on the drugs used by the medicine men. Eventually, the powers of certain drugs became highly guarded secrets known only to the men who governed their use.

It was not until the latter half of the nineteenth century that scientists began to make accurate experiments to discover precisely what chemicals were contained in drugs and what effect individual drugs might have in alleviating pain or curing disease. Before that, prescribing drugs was a hit-and-miss affair; physicians often ascribed wonderful curative properties to "patent medicines" that were worthless or harmful.

In the past 40 years, new drugs have revolutionized the practice of medicine. Since the development of sulfa drugs and antibiotics in the 1930s, hundreds of new drugs have been developed, many of them capable of reversing the course of a serious disease and saving an individual's life. Because of the development of these "wonder" drugs and their ready acceptance by the medical profession, many people have built up unrealistic expectations about what drugs can do for them. In other words, the people of the United States are, in general, "drug users." In their zealous search for miraculous cures, they too often decide for themselves what prescription drugs and what dosages they need instead of leaving this difficult and delicate decision where it belongs—in the hands of trained physicians. We feel that it is necessary for everyone to learn something about how drugs work. It is to be hoped that the more people know about drugs, the more cautious they will be regarding self-diagnosis, self-treatment, and the misuse of drugs.

How Drugs Work

After being taken into the body, drugs are distributed by the bloodstream to the many organs, tissues, and cells. The action or effect of a drug may be on the surface of cells, within the cell, or in the body fluids surrounding the cells. In most cases, the action takes place within the individual cells of the body and has a direct influence on the central nervous system. Drugs enter the cells in the same way that normal body chemicals do, usually because some part of the drug's chemical structure is similar to the structure of the normal body chemicals. This similarity allows the drugs to participate in a few stages of the normal sequence of common cellular processes. Ultimately, the differences between the drug and the normal chemical will be detected by the systems of the cell. But by this time the drug's work has been done. The cellular processes are no longer functioning normally; the cells, the organs, and the interrelated body systems are altered—the drug has taken effect.

How Drugs Are Given

Drugs enter the body orally, subcutaneously, intravenously, or by being inhaled into the lungs (Figure 1.1).

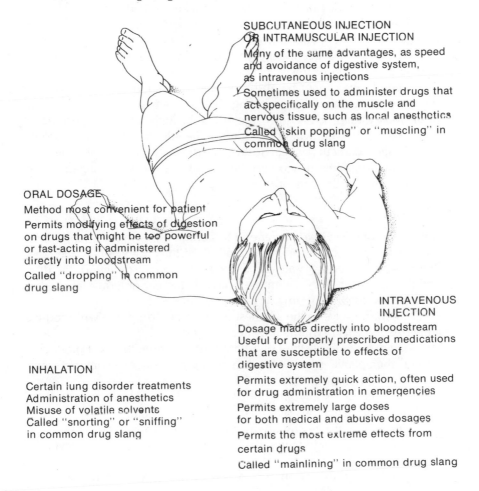

SUBCUTANEOUS INJECTION
OR INTRAMUSCULAR INJECTION

Many of the same advantages, as speed and avoidance of digestive system, as intravenous injections

Sometimes used to administer drugs that act specifically on the muscle and nervous tissue, such as local anesthetics

Called "skin popping" or "muscling" in common drug slang

ORAL DOSAGE

Method most convenient for patient

Permits modifying effects of digestion on drugs that might be too powerful or fast-acting if administered directly into bloodstream

Called "dropping" in common drug slang

INTRAVENOUS INJECTION

Dosage made directly into bloodstream Useful for properly prescribed medications that are susceptible to effects of digestive system

Permits extremely quick action, often used for drug administration in emergencies

Permits extremely large doses for both medical and abusive dosages

Permits the most extreme effects from certain drugs

Called "mainlining" in common drug slang

INHALATION

Certain lung disorder treatments Administration of anesthetics Misuse of volatile solvents Called "snorting" or "sniffing" in common drug slang

Only a doctor should decide how a drug ought to be administered. If he has a choice, he usually prefers to have an individual take a drug by mouth. Oral administration is convenient for the patient since he can take the drug at home without the aid of a doctor or nurse. Also, drugs taken orally assure a more gradual and sustained effect on the body, are not painful to take, and are less likely to produce adverse reactions.

When a doctor prescribes medicines to be taken by mouth, he usually specifies the time they should be taken, depending on the kind of action he desires. If he wants rapid action, he instructs the patient to take the drug *before* meals, so that the digestion of food will not interfere with the absorption of the drug into the bloodstream. If the medicine may irritate the stomach or if the doctor wants a slowed or sustained action, he usually instructs the individual to take it *after* meals. Drugs that produce sleep (hypnotic effect) or cause drowsiness are taken at bedtime.

The doctor's instructions often indicate *how long* a medicine should be taken to protect patients from needlessly dosing themselves after an illness has been brought under control or, on the other hand, from discontinuing the drug too early.

Some drugs cannot be absorbed into the bloodstream through the digestive tract. Others are irritating to that tract, while still others are destroyed by the gastric action of the stomach. Such drugs must be injected into a muscle or vein with a hypodermic needle. Injections may also be given when a particularly high dosage or extremely rapid action is desired.

Some drugs are inhaled into the lungs to treat certain lung disorders or to anesthetize the patient.

Drug Dosages

Any action or effect of a drug after it has entered the body depends upon the *dosage* used, that is, upon the amount of the drug given at one time. The dosage of a drug is calculated according to the strength of the drug and the actions it takes within the body. A number of terms are used to describe the amount of drug in a dose (Figure 1.2).

Minimal dosage is the smallest amount of a drug that will produce a *therapeutic effect* (will treat or heal someone).

Maximal dosage is the largest amount of a drug that will produce a desired therapeutic effect without producing any accompanying symptoms of *toxicity* (poisoning).

Toxic dosage is any amount of a drug that produces symptoms of poisoning and dangerous side effects in an individual.

Abusive dosage is any amount needed to produce the effects and actions desired by an individual abusing a drug. This is usually beyond a toxic amount.

Lethal dosage is any amount of a drug that will cause death.

Side Effects

Any drug powerful enough to be effective is potentially powerful enough to produce adverse reactions which are not always predictable. Individuals vary in the amount of drugs their bodies can tolerate. Doctors are very careful, and always conservative, about dosage when prescribing drugs. A responsible physician is often reluctant to prescribe new drugs

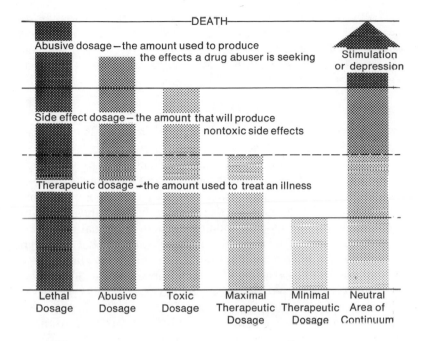

Figure 1.2 *Relative Dosages of Drugs*

that have not been widely used and thoroughly tested, partly because of the risk of undesirable side effects (see Figure 1.3).

Sometimes side effects are caused by the actions of drugs on organs other than those being treated. For example, antimalarial drugs may cause the whites of the eyes, or even the whole body, to turn yellow. Even as common a drug as aspirin can irritate the stomach and cause pain.

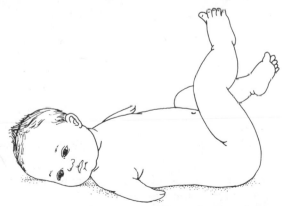

Figure 1.3 *Thalidomide baby. Thalidomide, a drug used as a tranquilizer or sedative in the early 1960s, was taken by a number of women while they were pregnant. Deformed children were born to many of these women.*

You should never take several drugs at one time unless the doctor has authorized it, since one drug can intensify the action of another. For example, alcohol greatly intensifies the action of barbiturates (sleeping pills), and death often results from even moderate amounts of both drugs taken at the same time.

Why and When Not to Take Drugs

Persons who visit a physician seeking relief from an illness sometimes respond with impatience and resentment when the doctor does not give them a prescription for drugs. But a doctor will not prescribe a medication until he knows exactly what he is treating, and the process of making a diagnosis may take time. If a doctor too quickly prescribes drugs that temporarily relieve the symptoms of an illness, he may interfere with the diagnostic procedure and risk endangering the individual.

Sometimes a physician does not prescribe drugs because he knows the disorder will correct itself without treatment or because he realizes that the patient needs reassurance more than medicine. Some diseases, such as the common cold, do not respond to drug treatment. Drugs taken for a cold (antihistamines, decongestants, etc.) can only alleviate the discomfort of the cold; they do not destroy the "germ" that causes the cold. Individuals who use an antibiotic such as penicillin for their colds have been misled: Colds are caused by viruses, and penicillin acts only on bacteria.

Physicians are even wary of using antibiotics against minor diseases that the antibiotics *can* help cure, since the risk of adverse reactions to antibiotics is always present. Also, the microorganism causing the disease can build up a resistance to the antibiotic. Then, later, the antibiotic will not be effective when it is needed to help cure a major—and perhaps otherwise fatal—illness.

What You Can Do   •

A doctor is the only person qualified to prescribe drugs in the treatment of illnesses. You can help yourself and assist your physician by following these rules:

1. Take drugs only in the amounts and at the times indicated by the doctor.
2. Immediately report to the doctor any adverse reactions to a drug.
3. Never try to treat illnesses on the basis of what you read, see on television, or hear from friends.
4. Take only those drugs that are prescribed specifically to treat a *present* illness. Your medicine chest should never contain "leftover" drugs.

Drug Abuse

Drugs have a legitimate and useful place in medical practice. But any drug can be abused, i.e., used for purposes other than those intended by a physician. When people speak of "drug use," they usually mean "drug misuse" or *drug abuse*. Abuse of drugs is usually associated with drug dosages many times in excess of those prescribed. *When a drug is self-administered in excessive dosages resulting in damages to an individual and/or society, the drug is being abused.*

In the past, certain commonly abused drugs were said to be "habituating" or "addicting." The explanations of these terms most often quoted today are those of the Expert Committee on Addiction-Producing Drugs of the World Health Organization. Table 1.1 compares these definitions. But the terms "addict" and "user" or "habitual user" do not always follow these definitions. An addict has been described as someone who is physically dependent upon the addicting drugs such as opium and its derivatives, synthetic narcotics, barbiturates, alcohol, and solvents. A user has been described as one who has a habituation for cocaine, amphetamines, marijuana, LSD, or other hallucinogenic drugs.

In fact, the terms "dependency," "drug dependency," "substance dependency," and "psychological dependency" express the situation

TABLE 1.1 Definitions of Addiction and Habituation

Drug Addiction	*Drug Habituation*
Drug addiction is a state of periodic or chronic intoxication produced by the repeated consumption of a drug (natural or synthetic). Its characteristics are:	Drug habituation is a condition resulting from the repeated consumption of a drug. Its characteristics are:
1. an overpowering desire or need (compulsion) to continue taking the drug and to obtain it by any means	1. a desire (but not a compulsion) to continue taking the drug for the sense of improved well-being or other effect it produces
2. a tendency to increase the dose (tolerance)	2. little or no tendency to increase the dose (little or no tolerance)
3. both psychic (psychological) and physical dependence on the effects of the drug and hence presence of abstinence syndrome (withdrawal illness)	3. some degree of psychic dependence on the effect of the drug, but absence of physical dependence and hence of abstinence syndrome
4. a detrimental effect on the individual and on society	4. detrimental effects, if any, primarily on the individual

Source: Modified from Maurice H. Seevers, "Medical Perspectives on Habituation and Addiction," *Journal of the American Medical Association*, 181, No. 2 (July 14, 1962), 92–98, Table 93.

more accurately. With the repeated use of *any substance* (food, tobacco, aspirin, alcohol, narcotics, etc.) some individuals develop a *dependence upon the substance*. The exact nature of this dependence varies with the type of substance being abused, the social acceptability of the substance (the differing degrees of acceptability of tobacco, alcohol, and heroin are examples), and the individual's reasons, social, emotional, or even political, for dependence upon the substance.

For instance, large amounts of food are consumed by individuals dependent upon food as an emotional stabilizer. Tremendous amounts of mild pain relievers (analgesics) with aspirin or aspirinlike ingredients are consumed every day. Tranquilizers, sedatives, and hypnotics are the most widely prescribed and consumed drugs in the United States and the world. Many individuals believe they cannot get up, do their work, keep their nerves under control, or go to sleep unless they have a pill to help them. There is a sound medical basis for temporary use of these drugs by many people and for permanent use by a few, but in general, such behavior is socially acceptable drug dependence.

Some drugs are "psychoactive," that is, alter the psychic state (mood, perception, consciousness), producing marked personality changes and abnormal social behavior. Such "mood modifiers" are abused because they cause *euphoria* (an extreme or exaggerated sense of pleasure or well-being), *hallucinations* (perceptions of unreal objects or, sometimes, false notions or illusions), or *recognizable changes in personality and behavior.*

Repeated consumption of some mood-modifying drugs can produce biochemical and physiological changes which may create physical drug dependence. With such drugs (those called "addicting"), the user must keep increasing the dosage to maintain the same mood-modifying effect. He is then said to have developed a *tolerance* for the drug. As his tolerance increases and he uses more of the drug, his body cells are gradually exposed to greater quantities of it. For a period of time the body will adjust to these slowly increasing amounts of the drug. However, it is always possible that the user will take a larger dose than his body can tolerate (a lethal dose) and will become extremely ill or die. If a drug-tolerant user suddenly stops taking drugs he will suffer from *withdrawal illness* or *abstinence syndrome,* as the cells of the body try to return to a normal drug-free life.

It is the psychoactive drugs and drugs that cause large numbers of deaths (for example, nicotine) that create problems for society.

Summary

I. Definition of drugs

   A. "Drug"—any substance, other than food, that alters the body or its functions

B. Actions and effects of drugs differ greatly

1. Some so mild effects almost imperceptible
2. Others so powerful they must be taken exactly as prescribed
3. Still others not even recognized by general public as drugs—caffeine, nicotine, alcohol, etc.

C. Some drugs considered "good drugs" when taken as prescribed and "bad" drugs when abused
D. In modern society word "drug" has vague and shifting meanings
E. Drug problems begin when chemicals used as means of problem-solving behavior

II. Medical use of drugs

A. How drugs work

1. Drugs are distributed by the blood stream
2. The action or effect of a drug may be:

a. On the surface of cells
b. Within cells
c. In the body fluids surrounding cells

B. How drugs are given

1. By mouth (orally)
2. By being injected into a muscle or vein
3. By being inhaled into the lungs

C. Drug dosages

1. Dosage of a drug is—the amount of a drug given to a person at one time
2. Dosage of a drug is calculated according to strength of drug and actions it will produce
3. A number of terms are used to describe the dosage of a drug—(see Figure 1.2)

D. Side effects

1. Any drug powerful enough to be effective is potentially powerful enough to produce adverse reactions
2. Side effects are not always predictable
3. Individuals also vary in the amount of drugs their bodies can tolerate

E. Why and when not to take drugs—a physician will not prescribe a medication until he knows exactly what he is treating
F. What you can do

1. Take drugs only in the amounts and at the times indicated by the doctor
2. Immediately report to the doctor any adverse reactions to a drug
3. Never try to treat illnesses on the basis of:

   a. What you read
   b. What you see on television
   c. What you hear from a friend

4. Take only those drugs that are prescribed specifically to treat a present illness
5. Your medicine chest should never contain leftover drugs

III. Drug abuse

A. When a drug is self-administered in abusive dosages and damages an individual, society, or both, the drug is being abused

   1. Terms "habituating" and "addicting" have become obsolete
   2. In their place one phrase should be used: *drug dependency*

B. Drugs that create problems within society are those that cause marked personality changes and abnormal social behavior

   1. Such drugs are called "mood modifiers"
   2. Mood modifiers are abused because they cause, in the user:

      a. Euphoria
      b. Hallucinations
      c. Recognizable changes in personality and behavior

Questions for Review

1. Distinguish between drug addiction, drug habituation, and drug dependency. Which term best describes repeated use of any drug?

2. What are the medically proper uses of a drug?

3. Is the amount of a drug used by an individual a factor in drug abuse?

4. What are your reactions to the statement by the authors that "The people of the United States, in general, are drug users"?

5. Are we a drug-using society?

Chapter 2

SUBSTANCES COMMONLY ABUSED

In the United States, over 20 million people use sleeping pills, over 10 million use diet pills (containing amphetamines or amphetaminelike substances), and over 50 million use tranquilizers. These numbers include those who have legal prescriptions for their drugs as well as the estimated illegal users. All of these substances are psycho-active drugs and modify the moods and behavior of these millions of individuals.

Depressants and Stimulants

In general, mood-modifying drugs act to increase or decrease the activity of nerve centers and their conducting pathways.

Depressant drugs temporarily depress a bodily function or nerve activity. Drug-induced depression of the central nervous system is fre-quently characterized by lack of interest in surroundings, inability to focus attention on a subject, and lack of motivation to move or talk. The pulse and respiration become slower than usual, and as the depression deepens, the ability to perceive sensations such as texture, sound, temperature, and pain diminishes progressively. Psychological and motor activities decrease; reflexes become sluggish and finally disappear. Depressant drugs are often quite accurately called "downers"; literally, they slow down the activity of the nervous system. If a strong depressant is used or if large (abusive) doses are consumed, depression progresses to drowsiness, stupor, unconsciousness, sleep, coma, and death.

A central nervous system *stimulant* is a drug that temporarily increases body or nerve activity. Stimulant drugs quickly produce a dramatic effect, but their medical usefulness is limited because of the complexity of their actions and the nature of their side effects. Such side effects may include hallucinations and delirium tremens. With repeated administration of abusive doses, convulsive seizures are often produced, alternating with periods of depression, coma, and exhaustion.

Continuum of Drug Actions and Effects

The action of depressant and stimulant drugs can be set into a continuum of effects and actions, as shown in Figure 2.1. This continuum of drug effects, suggested and formulated by Dr. Robert W. Earle of the University of California at Irvine, reaches to overstimulation and death at one extreme and to depression and death at the other. The neutral area of this continuum is the degree of stimulation and depression an individual encounters normally.

The drug groups are placed in Figure 2.1 according to the kind and degree of effects they produce when a normal therapeutic dose is consumed by an individual. Often drugs in different groups have similar actions. For example, narcotics are used to relieve pain, but they may also, as a side effect, cause drowsiness. Barbiturates are used for their ability to produce sleep, but they do not have the ability to relieve pain. Thus the sleep-producing effects of these two depressants, narcotics and barbiturates, overlap on the continuum chart (see Figure 2.2). In fact, many of the drugs that affect the central nervous system have similar actions. These overlapping actions were used by Dr. Earle to produce the continuum shown in Figure 2.1.

As we progress along the chart from the neutral area outward, we can locate the specific points where the effects of drugs overlap. These points show where the continuum moves from the major effective area of one group of drugs into the area of another more powerful group of drugs. The weaker drugs are nearer the center, while the most powerful drugs are at the two extremes.

If dosages are increased, any of the drug groups listed in Figure 2.1 may produce the complete range of effects of stimulation or depression. This overstimulation or extreme depression is the effect the drug abuser is seeking. Consequently, dosages used by drug abusers are far in excess of the dosages normally used in medical practice. The complete range of effects produced by increased dosages is represented in Figure 2.3.

The drug continuum in Figures 2.1, 2.2, and 2.3 serves to point out the fact that the extreme effects the drug abuser seeks are nearly always the

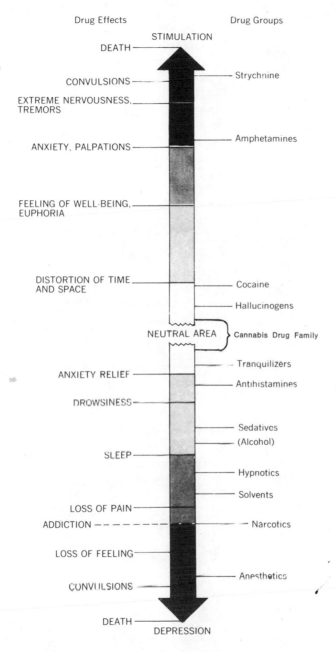

Figure 2.1 *Continuum of drug effects and actions. This graph shows the continuum of drug effects and actions when minimal doses of these drugs are used. (Courtesy of Robert W. Earle, Ph.D., Senior Lecturer, Department of Medical Pharmacology and Therapeutics, University of California, Irvine, California College of Medicine.)*

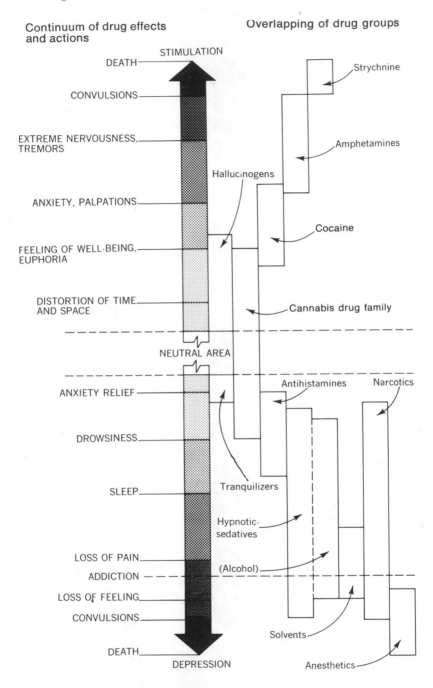

Figure 2.2 *Continuum of drug effects and actions, with overlapping effects of drug groups.*

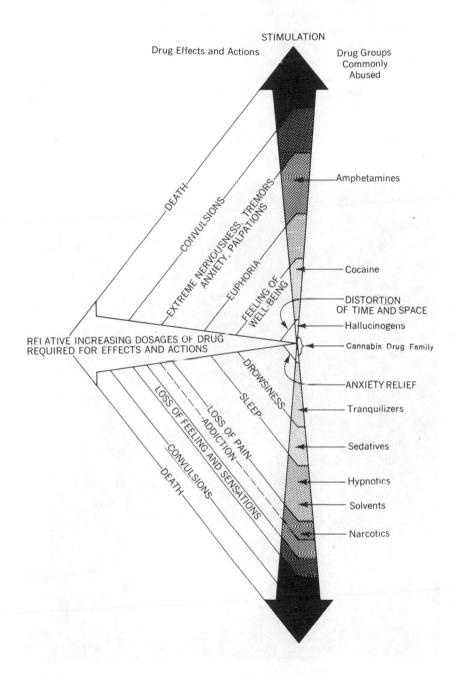

Figure 2.3 *Relationship of increased dosages to the continuum of drug effects. As the dosage of drugs is increased, the effects progress along a continuum of effects until a lethal dose is taken.*

same. For example, any of the stimulants will produce hallucinations if the dosage is strong enough (see Figure 2.2). This is why many individuals, while preferring one drug over another, will abuse any mood-modifying drug if it is available. As the specific actions of a drug become more familiar and less spectacular, the individual may experiment with new ways to use the drug. He may combine drugs of the same type or of different types to produce a more intense effect, a dangerous habit. He may progress from taking the drug orally to injecting it under the skin or into a muscle ("skin popping," see Figure 2.4) to injecting it directly into a vein ("mainlining," see Figure 2.5). The user may seek stronger and stronger drugs

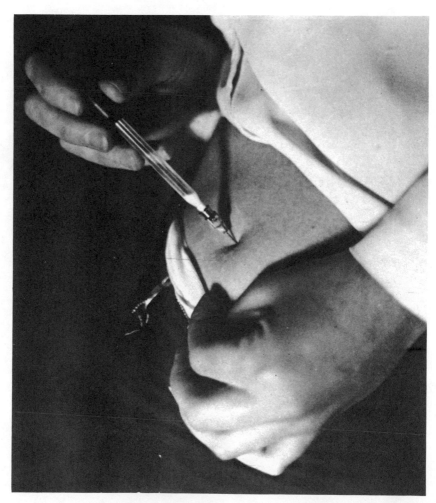

Figure 2.4 *"Skin pop." A girl injecting Methedrine ("speed") into the lower back. When a drug user cannot find or "raise" a vein to use for the injection, he will often inject into the skin or a muscle.*

to produce more vivid effects, quicker actions, or longer-lasting experiences. Very few drug abusers are satisfied with experiences from only one drug at one consistent dosage.

The more commonly abused drugs, such as marijuana or the barbiturates, are close to the center of the chart when used in small dosages. The strong preference for these drugs lies in the ability of an individual to control the amount and consequently the psychoactive effects of the drug. Many users of these drugs, particularly if they are not generally excitable or emotional, are contented with low dosages. On the other hand, highly emotional users or users seeking a specific "kick" are likely to increase the dosage and obtain a more intense effect. However, this ability to control drugs is offset, in the case of the depressant drugs, when *addiction*

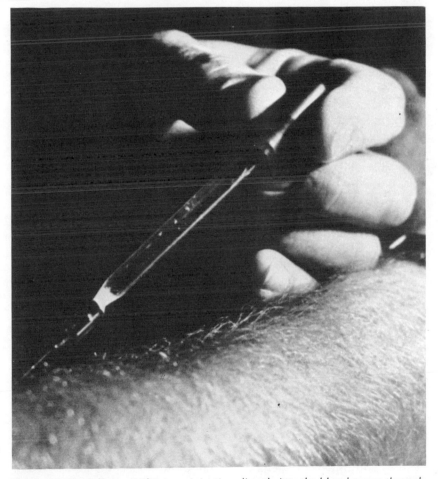

Figure 2.5 *"Mainlining." This is an injection directly into the bloodstream through a vein, which gives the desired effect immediately.*

levels are reached (see Figure 2.1). Then, regardless of the individual's desire or emotional state, a small but increasing dose is regularly required to keep the body from entering withdrawal. This increasing level must be reached daily to keep the individual performing at approximately the same level. Thus, he has built himself into a constantly changing continuum of effects.

Because stimulant drugs do not seem to have the clear-cut addictive properties of the depressants, many users never progress from the relatively mild drugs, such as marijuana, because they are able to control the effects they desire at a particular time. Others who start on the weaker drugs progress to stronger ones because they enjoy the slight differences of effects; some users, in seeking a more pleasurable reaction, eventually experiment with stronger drugs.

As already mentioned, each of these mood-modifying drugs either stimulates or depresses cellular functions. Caffeine, for instance, stimulates the nerve cells, while barbiturates depress them. Because of the complexity of the body's functions, drug action is often complex. At times, this complexity makes it extremely difficult to place a group of drugs on a progressive continuum chart such as that shown in Figures 2.1 and 2.2. Also, the complexity of a drug's action often leads to apparent paradoxes. For example, alcohol depresses the functioning of the brain. Why, then, do people seem stimulated rather than depressed by a small amount of alcohol? The answer is that one area in the brain acts as an inhibitor. Normally, this area keeps us from reacting indiscriminately to every impulse. This inhibitory center is more sensitive to alcohol and to similar drugs, such as barbiturates and solvents, than are the other centers of the brain. As the alcohol concentration in the blood begins to rise, the cells of the inhibitory center are depressed and cease to function properly, so that many impulses that would otherwise be suppressed are acted upon. Therefore, alcohol, a depressant drug, can initially cause excitation by depressing an inhibitory function.

Drugs Commonly Abused

Today much research on drugs is concerned with how they work in altering states of mind. Researchers are attempting to discover how certain chemicals work in modifying people's moods, personality, and behavior. During times of drug-induced behavioral changes, there may be a departure from rational or common-sense reasons for action. The girl who "gets into trouble" with a man—"But I had taken a tranquilizer and a sleeping pill and didn't know what I was doing"; "I attacked him while I was on speed"; "I'm usually a careful driver but those uppers made me go too fast"—these are examples of abnormal social behavior that create problems for individuals and for society.

Accordingly, it is wise to learn something about the mood-modifying or psychoactive drugs that are commonly abused. We will describe these drugs in 8 classifications: (1) narcotics, (2) volatile solvents, (3) hypnotic-sedatives, (4) tranquilizers, (5) cannabis-related drugs, (6) hallucinogenic compounds, (7) cocaine, and (8) amphetamines.

Narcotics[1]

The most widely abused drugs throughout the world, narcotics include *opiates* (opium and its derivatives) and synthetic narcotics (drugs chemically similar to opiates, but made in a laboratory from materials other than opium).

Narcotics work by depressing the body's central nervous system. Their effects include analgesia, sedation (freeing the mind of anxiety, relaxing the muscles, and calming the body), hypnosis, and euphoria. Narcotics are used in medicine primarily for their analgesic effect. Administered in controlled dosages, they cause insensitivity to pain without producing loss of consciousness or even excessive drowsiness. Doctors generally use *anesthetics,* or members of the hypnotic-sedative group, when they want to anesthetize patients for operations. They never use narcotics alone for this purpose, because narcotics used in large enough dosages to produce sleep or stupor could depress the respiratory center sufficiently to cause death.

An individual abusing a narcotic may develop a physical dependence on the drug; that is, he may become addicted to it. Because of the relatively weak preparations of narcotics sold illegally in the United States, some individuals ("chippies") can use narcotics off and on for years without ever becoming addicted. Tolerance to the drug develops quite rapidly. Then, when a person whose body has developed a tolerance has his supply of the drug cut off, a form of "withdrawal illness" called "narcotic-solvent abstinence syndrome" results. The intensity and nature of the symptoms vary with the type and strength of the narcotic abused. The symptoms of withdrawal from opium and its derivatives include irritability, depression, extreme nervousness, pain in the abdomen, and nausea—all to an agonizing degree.

Recognition of a narcotics addict, especially when he is regularly obtaining an increasing daily dosage, can be extremely difficult. He certainly does not want to give away the fact that he is an addict, and he is often, through experience, very clever at disguising it.

Very early in the process of addiction, before much tolerance has developed (see Table 1.1), the pupils of the eyes contract until they are

---

[1] The word "narcotic" is confusing because it is commonly used in at least three ways: (1) a narcotic is a depressant drug used to relieve pain, (2) it is an addicting drug, and (3) it is *any drug* that came under the restriction of the federal narcotics law (Harrison Narcotic Act) prior to passage of the 1970 Comprehensive Drug Abuse Prevention and Control Act.

"pinpointed" even in a weak, dim light whenever the addict is under the influence of a narcotic (see Figure 2.6). Unless he has also taken an antagonistic drug such as a stimulant, the addict's pupils will not react to light; that is, the pinpoint will not become smaller in a strong light even when it is flashed directly into the eyes, or larger (dilated) when the light is abruptly dimmed. In this condition, the eyes are said to be "frozen." After tolerance has begun to develop, the addict's pupils may begin to enlarge somewhat. When an addict has been without drugs for a short period of time (from 4 to 6 hours to overnight) and begins to enter withdrawal, his eyes become dilated (Figure 2.6) and exhibit a sluggish reaction to light. Again, however, this condition may be disguised by the effects of antagonistic drugs.

Under the influence of a stimulant drug, a user will have dilated, or enlarged, pupils that do not react to light.

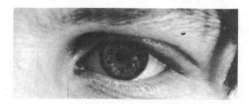

Normal pupil size.

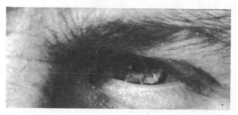

Under the influence of a depressant drug, the pupils show a contracted, pinpointed condition. These pupils do not react to light; i.e., the pinpoint does not change in strong light even if it is flashed directly into the eyes.

Figure 2.6 *Pupil reactions.* Top: *Dilated pupil reaction to a stimulant drug.* Middle: *Normal reaction in light of average intensity.* Bottom: *Contracted pupil reaction to a depressant drug.*

Owing to the depressant effects of narcotics, a user who has been addicted for a long time is often pale and emaciated. He may suffer from severe constipation. His appetite is poor. His sexual drive is usually reduced. While under the influence of a narcotic, he may be lazy, in a semi-stupor ("on the nod"), and dreamy. He is not particularly dangerous and certainly not violent. But if an addict is deprived of a regular narcotics supply (and he must have a "fix" every 4 to 6 hours), he may become dangerous. Addicts account for a vast majority of petty thievery, mugging, and prostitution in our large cities to obtain the money needed for drugs or the drugs themselves.

Some narcotics users start out by taking the drug orally. They will switch to injections when they learn—usually by associating with other users—that injections are more efficient. Then less of the drug is needed to obtain the effect wanted. A physician administering a narcotic usually gives a *subcutaneous injection* (see Figures 1.1 and 2.4). This method produces too slow an action for most addicts, who prefer to have an *intravenous injection* (see Figures 1.1 and 2.5). Because of the more rapid distribution throughout the body, an intravenous injection or "mainline" gives the desired effect immediately. Also, the effect is more prolonged.

The following are the major narcotics abused throughout the world.

OPIUM

Opium is the juice obtained from cutting the unripe capsule of the oriental poppy (*Papaver somniferum*) shown in Figure 2.7. This drug is generally smoked in an opium pipe or eaten. Because it is difficult to obtain, American drug abusers seldom use opium today, but there is great abuse of its derivatives, *morphine, heroin,* and *codeine,* which are the most important narcotic substances obtainable from opium.

MORPHINE   The major derivative from chemically refined opium is morphine. It may be pure white, light brown, or off-white in color and may come in the form of a cube, capsule, tablet, powder, or liquid solution. On the illegal market, morphine in a gelatine capsule is known as a "cap." The powder folded into a package is known as a "deck" or "package." Unlike heroin, very little morphine is sold on the streets. Rather, morphine addicts usually steal their supply from doctors' offices or pharmacies. Sometimes they obtain morphine by forging prescription forms that have been stolen from physicians.

HEROIN   Heroin is produced from morphine. In its pure state it is a grayish-brown powder. Because of its strength and the economics of illegal drug traffic it is diluted ("cut" or "hit") many times before it is sold on the street. Usually heroin is cut with milk sugar (lactose), mannite (a substance from the ash tree used as a mild laxative), and quinine. Often unsafe chemicals (such as strychnine, LSD, and amphetamines) are used as diluents during this cutting process. Street heroin ends up as a white or off-white powder, usually containing no more than 1 to 4 percent heroin.

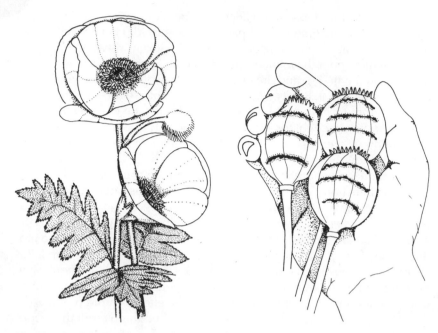

Figure 2.7 *Opium poppy.* Left: *Oriental (opium) poppy* (Papaver somniferum). *Since each plant yields little juice, large areas of poppies must be planted; most are grown profitably only in a hot, dry climate with cheap land and labor, such as India, Turkey, Egypt, and Mexico.* Right: *Workers harvest opium by making incisions into the capsules (pods) of the flowers, which cause the milky white juice of the pods to come to the surface during the cool of the night. As it comes in contact with the air, it oxidizes, thickens, and takes on a reddish-brown color. The next morning workers scrape off the new, heavy, molasseslike fluid and collect it on poppy leaves. This material gradually hardens, forming almost black gumlike balls. This is opium in its raw state; it has a bitter taste and a heavy, sweet odor.*

The main reason why laws controlling heroin have not been successful is the tremendous amount of money made each year by the illegal sale of heroin in the United States. Passing through five or six levels of distribution before reaching the user on the street, heroin is a billion-dollar product. For example, one kilogram (2.2 pounds) of heroin can be purchased for $5,000 to $10,000 by someone who has a "connection" with the individuals preparing the heroin from morphine. This "importer" has the heroin brought into the United States, dilutes it, and sells it to a "wholesaler" for $18,000 to $20,000. The wholesaler dilutes it again, dividing it into plastic bags containing about an ounce of cut heroin and selling these to local "dealers" for about $700 per bag. The wholesaler obtains about $32,000 for his bags. The dealer dilutes the heroin again and divides it into smaller portions called "pieces," "street ounces," or "vig ounces" ("vig" is a term used to describe the high interest charged by loan sharks). He packages these in folded squares of paper ("papers") or in clear or colored capsules ("caps") and sells these to the street "pusher." The dealer obtains about $70,000 for his product. After cutting the heroin or removing some for his own use, the pusher sells to the individual user at the street price, which varies at different times and in different cities. On the street the original single kilogram of heroin can return $225,000, producing $215,000 in profit.

CODEINE   Codeine is a relatively mild narcotic. The pure product is a white crystal powder which is sometimes taken in tablets for pain relief in combination with other ingredients (one such tablet is labeled "Empirin with codeine"). Codeine is also widely used as an ingredient in liquid cough medicines.

In many states, medicines containing a small amount of codeine (not more than one grain per ounce) can be sold over the counter without a prescription, but the pharmacist must keep a record of the purchaser's name. In some states, such medicines bear a label with the statement: "Contains codeine (opium derivative). WARNING—may be habit-forming. Do not give to children except upon advice of a physician."

Narcotics addicts sometimes resort to the use of codeine when deprived of their supply of stronger narcotics. Codeine is not widely abused because it is too mild to give a "hard" narcotic user, such as a heroin addict, the high he wants. Still, codeine, especially that found in some cough medicines, is often abused by young people when they can obtain it. It is an addictive drug, particularly when used frequently and in large amounts.

SYNTHETIC NARCOTICS

The synthetic narcotics differ from the opium derivatives and their compounds in that they are made synthetically in the chemical laboratory—not from opium, but from coal tar or petroleum products. Some of the more common synthetic compounds are Dilaudid, Percodan, Demerol, Percobarb, Methadone, and Nalline. Their chemical properties resemble those of various opium derivatives; their narcotic effect (and addictive potential) varies. But all narcotics, including synthetic ones, are addictive (see Figure 2.1).

Volatile Solvents (Glue)

The practice of inhaling vapors of volatile chemicals (see Figure 2.8), which has been widespread among young people, is also a major concern to society. Solvents from plastic or model airplane cement are inhaled for their mood-modifying effects. These effects primarily are feelings of pleasantness, cheerfulness, euphoria, and excitement—feelings that closely simulate the early stages of alcohol excitement. As a person inhales more, he begins to appear "drunk," exhibiting disorientation and speaking in a

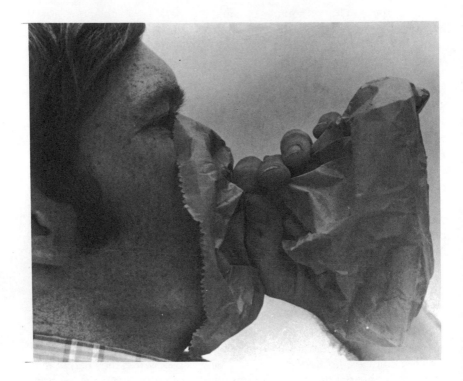

Figure 2.8 "Glue sniffing." The glue being sniffed is usually put either on a cloth (handkerchief, sock) or into a paper bag. The full face is put into the cloth or the bag and the vapors of the solvent inhaled.

slurred manner. Such behavior may continue for 30 to 45 minutes, followed by drowsiness, stupor, or unconsciousness. Unconsciousness may last for as long as an hour. If the person has inhaled too much glue, or if his exposure to the vapors has been prolonged, he may die.

Several toxic solvents are used in the manufacture of airplane cements. Common to many brands are isoamyl acetate and ethyl acetate. Other toxic solvents used in many products include benzene, toluene, and carbon tetrachloride. High concentrations of these solvents are found in cleaning fluids, paints, and paint thinners. Also, the hydrocarbons in gasoline (such as butane, hexane, and pentane) may cause solvent intoxication when inhaled. Prolonged inhalation of the fumes of any of these fluids may cause death. Labels on many types of solvents and gasoline include the warning "Use only in a well-ventilated, open area."

Tolerance to solvents develops rapidly, and the user soon finds he must inhale the vapors from the contents of several tubes of cement to experience the effects he desires. By this time he will have become addicted to the solvents (Figure 2.3).

An addicted glue-sniffer often has a characteristic, unpleasant odor to his breath. He may salivate excessively and spit frequently. The salivary secretions result from the solvent vapors' irritation of the mucous membranes of the nose and mouth. A user of glue may also suffer insomnia (inability to sleep), nausea, and weight loss.

The toxic effects of solvents have been carefully observed. They include irritation of the mucous membranes, the skin, and the respiratory tract; alternate excitation and depression of the central nervous system; cellular injury to the heart, liver, and kidneys; alteration of bone marrow activity, which results in anemia (reduction in red blood cells), leucopenia (reduction in white blood cells), and thrombocytopenia (reduction in platelets in the blood). There have also been reports of brain tissue deterioration, acute liver damage, and death from kidney failure.

With the abuse of solvents, there is a strong drug dependence, including severe mood-modifying effects and a quickly developed tolerance. This is why solvents are placed at such an extreme position in the continuum of drug effects shown in Figure 2.1.

Hypnotic-Sedatives

The group of hypnotic-sedative drugs is classified together because each drug has the ability to depress the central nervous system into a condition resembling sleep. The difference between a hypnotic action and a sedative action is one of degree of depression. A hypnotic drug, given in a moderate or even a small dose, will produce sleep soon after it is given. Such reduced dosages of sedative drugs, even when administered several times a day, will calm a person without producing sleep. With increasing dosages, all of the drugs in this group produce a continuum of effects from tranquilization to sedation (the allaying of excitement) to the loss of psychomotor efficiency to sleep, and then to coma and death (see Figure 2.1). The oldest hypnotic-sedative drug used in medicine was alcohol. For thousands of years the only hypnotic drugs man knew were alcohol and opium (now classified as a narcotic).

In 1864 a substance was produced by combining urea (an animal waste product) with malonic acid (derived from an acid in apples). The compound obtained, a new synthetic, was named "barbituric acid." Since then, chemists have produced more than 2,500 substances from barbituric acid. About 50 of these substances, with different *latency* (period of time between administration and effect) and *length of action* (period of time when the drug is effective), are marketed as *barbiturate drugs*.

BARBITURATES

The barbiturates are by far the most widely used and abused of all depressant drugs except alcohol. Doctors prescribe them mainly to help patients relax or sleep. Some commonly used and abused barbiturates and their properties are shown in Figure 2.9. On the illegal market, barbiturates are

Color and Shape of Capsule	Trade (and Generic Name)	Street Name	Chief Medical Use	Duration of Action
Blue-green 	Amytal (Amobarbital)	"Blue dragons"	Sedative and hypnotic	Intermediate
Red 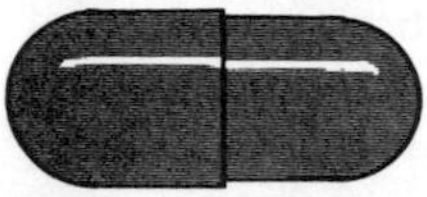	Seconal (Secobarbital)	"Reds" "Red birds" "Red devils"	Hypnotic	Short-acting
Red-blue 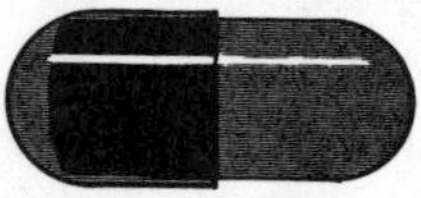	Tuinal (Combination of amobarbital and secobarbital)	"Rainbows"	Hypnotic	Moderately long-lasting
Yellow 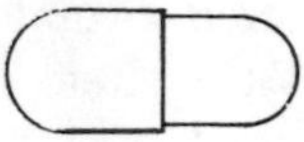	Nembutal (Pentobarbital)	"Yellow jackets"	Hypnotic sedative and anti-convulsant	Short-acting
Green 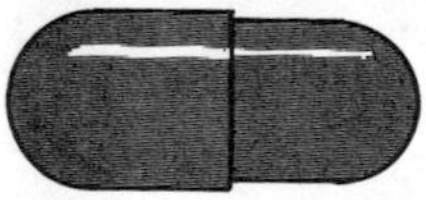	Luminal (Phenobarbital)	"Barbs"	Hypnotic	Long-acting

Figure 2.9 Commonly abused barbiturates, their lengths of action, names, and chief uses. About twenty of the several hundred barbituric compounds synthesized and tested are satisfactory for medical use. The barbiturates, which act on specific areas of the brain and which induce sleep promptly, are effective in treating conditions of anxiety, muscular twitching, delirium tremens, and convulsions. The compounds differ chiefly in the duration of their effect.

known as "sleeping pills," "goofballs," "reds" (because many are red in color), "downers," or "stumblers."

Barbiturates produce a surprisingly variable effect in the brain and nervous system of the person who uses them. After taking these drugs, many users undergo a short period of hyperactivity and excitement. Then, as the drug depresses their central nervous system, they become relaxed, euphoric, and sleepy. For some users, certain barbiturates produce a "truth serum" effect in which long-forgotten events are remembered. Also, a user may take a dose of barbiturates and discover that they seem to have no sedative or hypnotic effect at all because the period of hyperactivity and excitement has lasted throughout the night. With abusive dosages, drastic and sudden mood changes may occur; users are often described as "friendly one minute, mean the next."

Barbiturates are addictive drugs when abused. Drug dependence and tolerance develops quickly. They are usually taken orally ("dropped"); however, users can dissolve such compounds and inject them hypodermically. Sometimes they are dropped in combination with a stimulant such as Benzedrine, Dexedrine, or Methedrine (amphetamines; see page 35). This combination overcomes the depressing effects of the barbiturates and extends the excitement and euphoria. The use of a stimulant drug to antagonize the depressant effect of a barbiturate is extremely dangerous.

A risky practice indulged in by some persons who abuse barbiturates is to combine them with alcohol. Because the barbiturates interfere with the body's normal disposal of alcohol through the liver, the two drugs taken together have a total depressant effect far greater than the sum of their individual effects. Often, an overdose of either drug is taken unknowingly; the person is too drunk or too "doped up" to realize what he is doing. In any case, the use of alcohol and barbiturates in combination, even in small amounts, is extremely dangerous and too often results in death.

Since both are hypnotic-sedative drugs, the effects of barbiturates and alcohol are very similar. A small amount of barbiturates makes the user feel relaxed, sociable, and good-humored. He is also less alert than he normally is. After taking more of the drug, he may become sluggish, gloomy, and quarrelsome. His tongue becomes "thick," he staggers, and then gradually slumps into a deep sleep. If he has had a large amount of the drug, or if he has taken it in combination with alcohol, he may suddenly lapse into a coma. At this point, only prompt medical attention can save him. (Such attention has saved the lives of persons who showed no sign of life after lapsing into a barbiturate-induced coma.)

The effects of barbiturates and alcohol may be similar, but barbiturates are by far the potentially more lethal drug. It is difficult for a person to consume enough alcohol to cause death: His stomach rejects large amounts of alcohol, and he vomits after he has drunk a certain amount. But barbiturates are seldom vomited; instead, all of the drug taken into the stomach will be absorbed unless the stomach is pumped.

The chronic user of barbiturates, whether he takes the drug for its exciting and euphoric effects or because he must have it to sleep at night, finds that eventually he must increase the dosage to keep from going into withdrawal. Without a regular, daily dose, he will experience hallucinations and convulsive seizures that resemble grand mal epileptic convulsions. The convulsions are sometimes severe enough to cause death. These symptoms and the delirium tremens experienced by alcoholics withdrawing from alcohol are termed "alcohol-barbiturate abstinence syndrome."

NONBARBITURATE HYPNOTIC-SEDATIVES

There are a number of hypnotic-sedative drugs, other than alcohol, that produce reactions similar to barbiturates. Many of these drugs are very strong depressants and are at least as dangerous as the barbiturates. On the continuum of drug actions their effects often dip into the level of the anesthetics.

Quaalude (methaqualone), also known as "ludes," or "soapers," has been the most widely abused of this group. Because Quaalude produces a prolonged feeling of euphoria without the initial excitement phase of barbiturates, many individuals erroneously believe that it is not dangerous and does not cause dependency. Quaalude is also mistakenly believed to stimulate sexual drive. Any hypnotic-sedative reduces inhibitions, leading to a freer feeling toward sexual activity, but Quaalude does not reduce inhibitions any more than alcohol. Withdrawal from methaqualone, because of its strength, can cause severe delirium tremens and convulsions. "Luding out" can cause death, especially when methaqualone is taken with other depressants, such as alcohol.

Other members of this group are Glutethimide (Doriden or "Ciba") and phencyclidine (Sernyl), which is also called "PCP," "hog," "angel dust," or "the peace pill."

Tranquilizers

The tranquilizing drugs are able to relieve or prevent uncomfortable emotions. They are used to relieve tension and apprehension and produce a state of calm and relaxation. The tranquilizers are divided into two distinct groups, each with its own properties and uses.

The *major tranquilizers,* so called bacause they are potent drugs used by psychiatrists in helping persons with major mental illnesses, produce dramatic effects in calming and handling violent, overactive, psychotic individuals. They do not cure mental illness, but they make it easier for psychiatrists to manage mentally ill patients. The most commonly used major tranquilizers are the phenothiazines (chlorpromazine, thioridazine, promazine), butyrephenones, thioxanthenes, and reserpines.

Minor tranquilizers are widely used among the general public to combat anxiety and the symptoms that often accompany it, including fast heartbeat, tension, headaches, gastrointestinal disturbances, restlessness, insomnia, and irritability. Tranquilizers have the specific ability to calm an individual without producing extreme depression or upsetting the abilities to function physically. The better-known minor tranquilizers include meprobamate (Equanil, Miltown), hydroxyzine (Atarax, Vistaril), chlordi-azepoxide (Librium), and diazepam (Valium).

A combination of Librium and Valium, called "flying saucers," is being abused on the West Coast. But the greatest abuse comes from individuals using larger quantities than their doctors prescribe, in which case sudden abstinence or unavailability can cause extreme nervousness and other symptoms of drug withdrawal. Dr. Ismet Karacan, Associate Chief of Staff Research for the Veterans Administration, has found abnormal electrical activity in the brain for months after withdrawal from minor tranquilizers.

Individuals who use the minor tranquilizers in prescribed dosages usually experience no adverse effects from the drugs themselves or from withdrawal of the drug.

Cannabis-Related Drugs (Marijuana)

The cannabis drug family has been well-known since ancient times. The drugs are produced from the many varieties of *Cannabis sativa* (Figure 2.10) grown throughout the world. The leaves and flowering tops of the

Figure 2.10 *A full-size, mature marijuana plant.*

female plant contain an amber-colored resin called cannabine, cannabinol, or tetrahydrocannabinol, which is the psychoactive substance causing the mood modifications and behavior changes in the user. The potency
of the drugs produced from the cannabis plant—marijuana, hashish,
charas, THC—varies widely, depending upon the variety of plant being
used, which parts of the plant are used (stems, roots, and seeds do not contain tetrahydrocannabinol), the method of preparation, and how the drug is
stored until it is used. This drug family, more than any other, cannot be
accurately discussed without specifying dose levels.

Marijuana, used mostly in the United States, is probably the weakest
preparation of the plant used in the world. The strongest preparation, used
mainly in India, is charas, the unadulterated tetrahydrocannabinol resin
obtained from the female plant or its dried flowers. Hashish is a powdered
and sifted form of charas. Hashish, or "hash," and "hash-oil" are being
sold in the United States. A synthetic form of tetrahydrocannabinol called
"THC" has been produced. It has been used in scientific studies and has
been found to be weaker than the naturally occurring tetrahydrocannabinol. There have been reports of THC being available on the street, but
this is unlikely because of its extremely high cost. When tested, the street
THC has been found to consist mainly of combinations of substitute drugs
—often hallucinogens and amphetamines. None of the liquid forms of
street THC is pure, and often such mixtures of various unknown chemicals
can be very dangerous.

Tetrahydrocannabinol in large doses, such as in hashish, produces
reactions (hallucinations, distortion of time and space, etc.) similar to the
hallucinogenic drugs. A mild form of the drug, such as marijuana, when
used in low "social" doses, is quite different, and the effects tend to
approximate mild intoxication with alcohol (a depressant). The cannabis
drug family has been placed across the neutral area of the drug continuum, shown in Figure 2.1, because of its wide range of actions and
effects. This range varies with the form of the drug used (marijuana or hashish), the emotional state and personality of the user, social factors, and the
dosage used. If an individual uses a strong form (such as hashish) or consumes a large number of marijuana cigarettes, his reactions tend toward
the stimulant end of the continuum of drug actions (Figure 2.11, line A).
If a "social dose" (part of a cigarette or one or two cigarettes) is taken, the
user's reactions are more closely tied to the emotional and social variables
present. As shown in Figure 2.11, line B, if the individual is stimulated (by
music, colored lights, etc.) the reaction will be a slight depression causing
him to relax, release tension, and enjoy the situation. But if he continues to
consume the drug (broken section of line B) he will tend to feel its stimu-
lating effects. If the individual is emotionally depressed to begin with, he
will be stimulated by any dose of the drug (line C).

Physical reactions to cannabinol may include quickening of the
pulse, dilation of the pupils, dry mouth and throat, and increased hunger

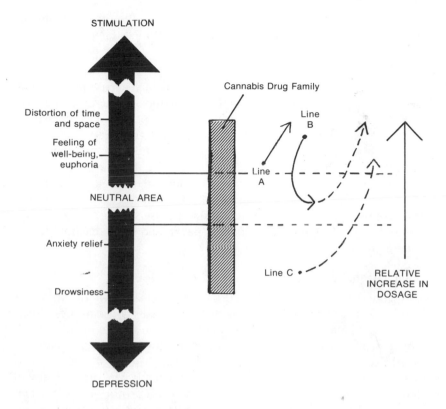

Figure 2.11 *Relative effects of potency and drug dosage in cannabis drugs.*

and thirst. If cannabinol is smoked, the effect occurs almost immediately because the drug is absorbed directly through the lungs. If it is eaten, the effect is delayed but more sustained.

MARIJUANA

Marijuana is usually rolled into cigarettes, or "joints," and smoked. It cannot be confused with tobacco, being green rather than brown and having a different (alfalfa- or tealike) smell.

Often a new marijuana user does not experience any effect from the drug until he has tried it several times, on several different occasions, over a period of weeks. After he has "turned on" once to marijuana, however, he usually feels some effect almost every time he uses it. The effects vary greatly and depend upon many factors. A social dose sometimes produces simply a feeling of well-being, a euphoric effect. If a smoker is alone, he may choose to sit quietly and observe the world around him—the room he is in, cars going by in the street, people strolling by, or flowers and leaves. In a group, he may be talkative and may feel close to the others with whom he is turning on. Music may sound especially meaningful and food taste exceptionally good. His senses of touch and perception may be altered, and his concepts of time and space may be distorted (Figure 2.1).

HASHISH

Individuals using potent extracts from cannabis plants experience distortions of hearing and sight, sometimes hallucinations, and a sense of depersonalization similar to that occurring with the use of LSD. Tolerance does develop when high dosages are used over prolonged periods, but there is no cross-tolerance (tolerance to one drug produced by some other drug) with any of the hallucinogenic drugs such as LSD or mescaline. The effects of even large dosages of hash are milder and more easily controlled than hallucinogens. The differing "trips" or "highs" caused by the two classes of drugs are readily distinguishable by users; hashish users, even at high dosages, lack the major anxiety, panic, and stress reactions found in hallucinogen users.

Hallucinogenic Compounds

Hallucinogens (see Figure 2.1) are drugs which create vivid distortions of the senses without greatly disturbing the individual's consciousness. Such distortions, "hallucinations," may cause a person to see, hear, or smell things that are not really there. Or, he may view the world much differently from the way it really is (or from the way he usually views it). Persons who abuse the hallucinogens may share with individuals who are mentally ill a tendency to experience hallucinations when they do not want to or when they are no longer under the influence of a drug. This is why some hallucinogens have been termed "psychotomimetic" (psychosis-mimicking) or "psychotogenic" (psychosis-producing) drugs. Such drugs, some authorities feel, are capable of temporarily turning a normal person into a psychotic. It is true that users have often been hospitalized to prevent them from doing harm to themselves or others during what seems to be such a temporary psychosis.

During recent years, psychiatrists have been increasingly interested in hallucinogenic drugs. Some have taken doses of these compounds themselves in order to experience something of what their severely ill psychiatric patients must feel. Other researchers, influenced by colleagues who have described these hallucinogenic drugs as "psychedelic," "mind-realizing," or "mind-expanding," have tried using them in an attempt to gain insight into their own minds. Finally, these drugs have been given to alcoholics and other emotionally disturbed patients as a part of therapeutic treatment. The results of these experiments have been contradictory, and in general they have not borne out the expectations of the investigators.

A large number of people acquire these drugs illegally and take them without medical supervision, sometimes while participating in cultlike group experiences. Occasionally a severe psychotic reaction or a prolonged delirious reaction follows the use of hallucinogens. Psychiatrists report that they are frequently called upon to give emergency help to persons who are suffering "bad trips" ("bummers") from these drugs.

Hallucinogens important in today's news include mescaline, a drug obtained from the peyote cactus plant *(Lophophora williamsii);* LSD, a synthetic drug based on lysergic acid diethylamide, a chemical which in turn is derived from ergot (a black fungus that grows on rye and wheat); DMT (dimethyltryptamine); bufotenin, originally isolated from the skin of toads; and CI-395 (phencyclidine).

MESCALINE

Mescaline is named after the Mescalero Apaches, who developed a cult *RELigion* that involved using the drug in religious rituals. Mescaline is found in the small, buttonlike peyote cactus plant (Figure 2.12), which grows naturally

Figure 2.12 *Peyote (Lophophora williamsii). This small, buttonlike cactus plant, which normally grows in the watershed of the Rio Grande River, produces mescaline.*

in the watershed of the Rio Grande. Indians in the southwestern United States chew the cactus in order to experience hallucinatory states as part of religious ceremonies. Considerable controversy has developed in the past several years over whether the United States government should or should not permit such drug use. At present the government feels that the constitutionally guaranteed right of freedom of religion would be denied if these Indians were forbidden use of peyote in religious ceremonies.

The peyote plants are usually dried and then chewed. Sometimes they are boiled in water to make a broth. Mescaline causes hallucinations and euphoria lasting between 8 hours and 2 days. These hallucinations may include the appearance of fantastic geometric patterns, distortions in the sense of time and space, and feelings of depersonalization.

LSD

Commonly referred to by users as "acid," LSD is a tasteless, colorless, and odorless drug derived from lysergic acid diethylamide. The primary danger in taking LSD is that it may cause temporary psychosis, accompanied by almost any sort of behavioral disturbance. Some users experience panic or depression, while others feel euphoria and a sense of great mental clarity or comprehension. Visual hallucinations are commonly experienced.

An LSD trip lasts 8 to 16 hours. Afterward, users who have enjoyed their trip may describe a feeling of having been reborn, of having seen the world for the first time. This feeling is often accompanied by a sense of deep affection for others, particularly those who were present and participating in the trip.

Doses of LSD are measured in micrograms; an average dose can be anywhere from 150 to 250 micrograms. A user taking much larger doses may experience delirium and convulsions. After any dose, "flashbacks" may occur; that is, the psychotic effects of the drug may recur from time to time up to a year or more after the trip.

LSD dilates the pupils and raises the blood pressure. It stimulates the brain's sensory centers and blocks off its inhibiting mechanisms. It intensifies hearing, increases the ability to differentiate among textures, and may produce a tingling sensation and numbness of the hands and feet. Subjects often report crossovers of sensation; for example, they may seem to hear colors or smell the scent of music.

Cocaine

Cocaine has a depressing effect only when it is used as a local anesthetic; its general effect on the body is to stimulate and induce excitement. Though not addictive, it produces a strong psychological dependence.

Cocaine, or "coke," is prepared from the coca plant (Figure 2.13) and processed into an odorless, white, fluffy, fine crystalline powder. On the criminal market, it is sometimes referred to as "snow" because of its

Figure 2.13 *Coca plant* (Erythroxylon coca). *Cocaine is extracted from the flowering branch of this shrub or small tree, which grows to 12 or 15 feet and is found in Peru and Bolivia.*

appearance. It is sold in the same types of containers as heroin. But the price is always quite high because cocaine is more difficult to obtain than heroin.

Cocaine users usually sniff the drug into their nostrils. A few users take the drug by hypodermic injection. Sniffing is the more popular method because, when the drug is absorbed slowly through the membranes of the nose, its effects last longer and are less violent than when it is injected. Narcotic addicts may mix cocaine and heroin together. This combined injection is called a "speedball."

Amphetamines

Included in the stimulant group are a large number of drugs which mimic the actions of adrenaline (epinephrine). In general, the physical reactions they produce are an increase in heart rate, constriction of certain blood vessels, an increase in blood pressure, dilation of the pupils, an increase in the breathing rate, an increase in sweating, and a cottonlike dryness in the mouth. These side reactions are always combined with the primary actions of amphetamines on the brain: an increase in bodily activity and an elevation of mood. Feelings and behavior aroused by amphetamines include increased confidence, euphoria, fearlessness, talkativeness, impulsiveness, loss of appetite, and decrease of fatigue.

A large number of amphetamine drugs on the market are mainly used for weight reduction (diet pills). The most widely abused amphetamines, Benzedrine and Dexedrine, are often prescribed for this purpose. On the illegal market they are known as "bennies," "dexies," "pep pills," or "whites" (because Benzedrine is sold as a white tablet), or as "uppers" and "leapers" (because of the mood elevation; Figure 2.14). Several drug companies, without showing substantial evidence, make claims that their particular compound suppresses the appetite without causing central nervous system stimulation. No amphetamine or amphetaminelike compound has only one of these two actions on the body. Consequently, the usual circumstance is that while the user loses weight, he also loses sleep.

Actually, many of the chronic users of "pep pills" give a desire for weight loss as an excuse for taking these drugs. Amphetamines produce weight loss by making people active and suppressing their appetite. If they continue to take more, they can keep going for hours or even days without sleep or rest. Consequently, these drugs are sometimes abused by those who want to work or play harder or longer than their normal capacities allow them to.

There are several ways in which these drugs can cause physical damage when they are used over long periods of time. The mechanism in the liver which activates amphetamines is destroyed or impaired quite quickly; therefore, users have to increase dosage levels continually to maintain the desired effectiveness. Prolonged use of increasing dosages causes long periods of sleep loss and mood and behavior changes, which may develop into a severe mental disorder or psychosis. The people suffering from this mental disorder are usually characterized by extreme activity for long periods of time, feelings of superiority, bizarre forms of suspiciousness, hallucinations, and excitement—all to an exaggerated degree. Those that suddenly stop using amphetamines (often because these drugs have stopped being effective) usually go through a rather prolonged period of lethargy, depression, nightmares, and restlessness.

Young people particularly are abusing amphetamines for their mood-modifying qualities, often together with barbiturates or alcohol. Such abuse is physically dangerous; it can cause death or lead to impulsive acts of poor judgment and to accidents. Especially abused is the amphetamine compound Methedrine (methamphetamine hydrochloride), commonly called "speed" or "meth." Some people swallow Methedrine pills, but the majority inject the compound into a muscle ("skin pop," Figure 2.4) or vein ("mainline") to get a quick euphoric "flash" or "rush." With continued injections, they will stay awake for days and eat very little, until

Trade Names	Color and Shape of Capsule or Tablet		Street Names
Benzedrine (spansule capsule)	Red-pink		"Bennies"
Benzedrine (tablet)	Pink		"Bennies"
Dexedrine (spansule capsule)	Orange		"Dexies"
Dexedrine (tablet)	Orange		"Dexies"
Dexamyl (tablet) (contains Dexedrine and amobarbital)	Green		
Edrisal (tablet) (contains Benzedrine, aspirin, and phenacetin)	White		
Biphetamine (capsule)	White		"Whites"
Methedrine (tablet)	White		"Meth" "Speed" "Crystals" "Whites"

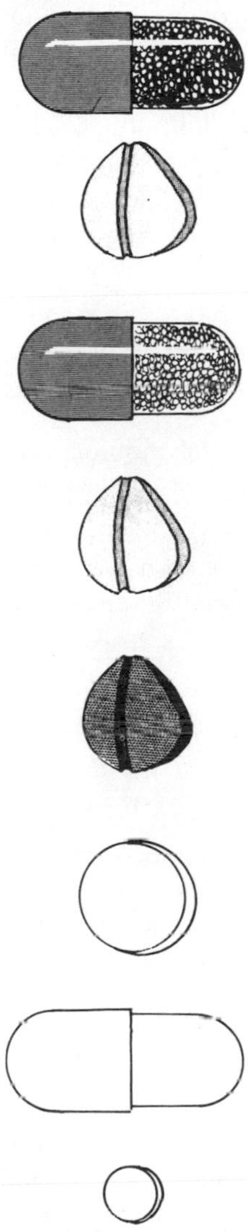

Figure 2.14 *Amphetamines. The primary effects of the many brands of amphetamines—available in white or colored tablets or timed disintegration capsules—are an increase in confidence, euphoria, feelings of fearlessness, talkativeness, impulsive behavior, loss of appetite, and decrease in fatigue. Variously called "leapers," "uppers," "beans," "pep pills," and "diet pills," they produce strong psychological dependence.*

their bodies become completely exhausted ("strung out"). Then the worst part of a "speed trip" begins, the withdrawal from the drug, or "crashing." Heavy users stop their injections, slip between coma and sleep for days, then awaken and start their injections again.

A great danger from amphetamines is the effect they have on automobile drivers. When a number of pills are taken at one time, or if they are used for a long period of time without rest or sleep, they may produce hallucinations or delirium. Users may feel that someone or something in another automobile is following them, or they may black out suddenly while driving at high speeds. These effects are so dangerous that many states have made it a *felony offense to drive while under the influence of amphetamines.*

Summary

I. Depressants and stimulants

A. Mood-modifying drugs act to increase or decrease the activity of nerve centers and their conducting pathways

1. *Depressant* drugs have the ability to temporarily depress a bodily function or nerve activity
2. *Stimulant* drugs have the ability to temporarily increase body or nerve activity

B. Continuum of drug actions and effects

1. The degrees of depression and stimulation of drugs affecting the central nervous system are not interconnected actions.

a. The continuum of drug effects reaches from overstimulation to death at one extreme, and depression to death at the other
b. The "neutral area" is the degree of stimulation and depression an individual encounters normally

II. Drugs commonly abused

A. Narcotics

1. The most widely abused drugs throughout the world
2. These include *opiates,* and synthetic narcotics (drugs chemically similar to opiates, but made in a chemical laboratory from materials other than opium)
3. Narcotics work by depressing the body's central nervous system
4. Individuals abusing narcotics develop a physical dependence to the drug (tolerance) and are said to be "addicted" to the drug
5. If the supply of the drug is cut off after the developoment of a tolerance, a condition called narcotic-solvent *withdrawal illness* results

6. Some narcotics users begin by taking the drug orally but switch to injections

7. The major narcotics abused throughout the world are:

    a. Opium

        (1) Obtained from extracts of the oriental poppy *(Papaver somniferum)*

        (2) Because it is difficult to obtain, American drug abusers seldom use opium today

    b. Morphine

        (1) The major opiate derivative produced from opium

        (2) Very little morphine is sold on the streets

    c. Heroin

        (1) Produced from morphine

        (2) Considered the most dangerous of the narcotic drugs

    d. Codeine, a relatively mild narcotic

    e. Synthetic Narcotics

        (1) They are synthetically produced chemicals

        (2) Their narcotic effects are variable

        (3) All are addicting

B. Volatile solvents

    1. These are all toxic solvents, such as:

        a. Isoamyl acetate

        b. Ethyl acetate

        c. Benzine

        d. Toluene

        e. Carbon tetrachloride

    2. These are inhaled because of their mood-modifying effects

    3. The toxic effects have been carefully observed

    4. A strong drug dependence develops with the abuse of solvents

C. Hypnotic-sedative drugs

    1. These drugs are classified together because each drug has the ability to depress the central nervous system into a condition resembling sleep

    2. The difference between a hypnotic action and a sedative action is one of degree of depression

    3. Alcohol—the oldest hypnotic-sedative used in medicine

    4. Barbiturates

        a. Most widely used hypnotic-sedative

b. Sudden removal forces an addict into severe withdrawal—producing seizures resembling epileptic convulsions, often severe enough to cause death
c. On the illegal market, are known as "sleeping pills," "goof-balls," "reds," "downers," or "stumblers"

5. Nonbarbiturate Hypnotic-Sedative Substances—many are very strong depressants and effects dip into the level of anesthetics (see Figure 2.2)

D. Tranquilizers

1. The major tranquilizers

a. Called major tranquilizers because they are strong drugs used by psychiatrists and other medical practitioners in helping persons with major mental illnesses
b. Their effects on normal individuals vary, but they can cause feelings of depression or produce deep sleep

2. The minor tranquilizers

a. These drugs are used to combat anxiety and the symptoms that often accompany it (fast heartbeat, tension headaches, etc.)
b. Tranquilizers are widely used among the general population
c. Few of the minor tranquilizers are commonly used illegally because they do not produce exaggerated euphoria or marked mood-modifying effects
d. Some persons do use tranquilizers in larger quantities than prescribed—resulting in drug abuse

E. Cannabis drug family

1. Drugs produced from the plant *Cannabis sativa*
2. This drug family, more than any other, cannot be accurately discussed without specifying dose levels (see Figure 2.1)
3. Marijuana—leaves of the plant rolled into cigarettes
4. Hashish—potent extracts from cannabis plant

F. Hallucinogenic compounds

1. Hallucinogens are drugs which create vivid distortions of the sense without greatly disturbing the individual's consciousness
2. Hallucinogens important in today's society include:

a. Mescaline
(1) Found in the buttonlike, small peyote cactus plant
(2) The peyote plants are usually dried and then chewed; they may be boiled in water and made into a broth
(3) Mescaline, which is extracted from peyote buttons, is available on the illegal market in capsule form

b. LSD

(1) LSD is a tasteless, colorless, and odorless drug derived from *lysergic acid diethylamide*
(2) The primary danger with this drug is that it may cause temporary psychosis, accompanied by almost any sort of behavioral disturbance
(3) Large doses of LSD may cause delirium and convulsions. After any dose, flashbacks may occur; that is, the psychotic effects of the drug may recur from time to time up to a year or more

G. Cocaine

1. Prepared from the leaves of the coca plant
2. An odorless, white, fluffy, fine crystalline powder
3. The drug is usually sniffed into the nostrils

H. Amphetamines

1. A group of stimulant drugs which mimic the actions of adrenalin on the sympathetic nervous system
2. On the legal market a large number of amphetamine drugs are mainly used for weight reduction (diet pills)
3. Prolonged use of increasing dosages causes long periods of sleep loss and mood and behavior changes, which may develop into a severe mental disorder or psychosis

Questions for Review

1. While opium is seldom used by drug addicts, its derivatives are. What are the opiate derivatives and how are they used?

2. Which drugs are physically addicting?

3. Many individuals believe that marijuana should be legalized. State why you would be for or against such legislation.

4. What are the general effects of stimulants and depressants upon the body?

5. Explain the placement of drugs on the *Continuum of Drug Actions and Effects*

Chapter 3

THE PSYCHO-SOCIAL PROBLEM OF DRUG ABUSE

It is becoming increasingly evident that people with problems—emotional and social—abuse drugs. No one will continue to do something that does not provide him with at least some satisfaction. The reasons for abusing substances are complex but are basically the same whether the person uses marijuana, alcohol, hallucinogens, narcotics, barbiturates, amphetamines, tranquilizers, aspirin, nicotine, or caffeine. The individual wants to change the pace of life, to modify moods, to reduce anxiety, to increase activity, to relieve tension, to relieve boredom, to facilitate social interactions, to sleep, or just to have "fun."

Drug Abuse Behavior

Not everyone who explores the effects of mood-modifying substances (legal and illegal) will follow the same predictable pattern of behavior. But all individuals introduced to such substances will fall within one or more of the following categories of drug behavior.

Categories of Drug Abusers

EXPERIMENTERS

Well over half of all individuals who are reported to be "drug users" turn out to have "used drugs"—often not more than three times—and have no intention of using illegal drugs again. Such people, in reality, are *drug experimenters* and *tasters*. They have no place in a discussion of drug abuse because they have already made their decision not to use drugs.

OCCASIONAL USERS

Many individuals during their experimentation with drugs find they need and enjoy the social, personal, and emotional gratification that mood-modifying drugs give them. They continue their experimentation with drugs and may be called *occasional* users. These individuals are extremely socially conscious and use the current "in" or "cool" drugs. When the drug is alcohol, these individuals are called "social drinkers" who enjoy partying. A very fine line divides the occasional user from the regular user.

REGULAR USERS

Some individuals use drugs regularly, that is, one or more times per week. It is with such users that a discussion of drug abuse problems properly begins. Regular users often experiment with a variety of different drugs and are "in-drug" users. To them, drugs are part of a general "turned-on" ideology and a membership card in a life-style or subculture. Depending on the drug, regular users are called "heads," "potheads," "coke heads," "acidheads," "weekend drunks," "periodic alcoholics," or "problem drinkers."

These individuals are often the greatest defenders of the personal right to use drugs. They have very closed minds concerning drugs because of *street experimentation*—"I know, because I have been there"—a very dangerous type of experimentation. The most dangerous aspect of regular drug use is that of falling into an apparently self-destructive life-style. This results in personality deficiencies and emotional problems that may restrict the individual's ability to deal constructively with the problems of life. At this point the individual is considered a compulsive drug user.

COMPULSIVE DRUG ABUSERS

Compulsive drug abuse (addiction or alcoholism) is always associated with an abnormal personality (an addictive personality), and the individual is emotionally ill. Compulsive drug abusers use drugs as their means of coping with the stresses of the environment. Whenever stress is placed upon such an individual, he turns to drugs, and under their influence his personality shifts, abnormal social behavior, and modified moods are often very dramatic. An excellent example of compulsive drug abuse is *alcoholism*.

What Is Alcoholism?

There is no clear-cut, widely accepted definition of the word "alcoholism." Some people suggest such a simple definition as: "An alcoholic is someone who drinks too much." But what is "too much" drinking? Probably everybody has a different opinion. A better general definition is, "An alcoholic is someone whose drinking interferes with a useful life." An important point is suggested here: The way to determine if someone is an alcoholic is not to measure how much he drinks, but to observe what effect his drinking has on his life.

There are also more restrictive definitions of alcoholism, such as the one given by Doctors Chafetz and Demone in their book *Alcoholism and Society* (New York, Oxford University Press, 1962):

> [Alcoholism is] a chronic behavioral disorder manifested by undue preoccupation with alcohol to the detriment of physical and mental health, by a loss of control when drinking has begun (although it may not be carried on to the point of intoxication), and by a self-destructive attitude in dealing with relationships and life situations.

Early Signs of Alcoholism

No one ever decides to become an alcoholic. Almost every new drinker assumes that he will always be able to handle liquor—and he is almost always right. But there is no way to predict which drinker will be the one out of every fourteen who does develop the disease of alcoholism. The great majority of those becoming alcoholics do not even realize what is happening to them until it is too late to stop.

Fortunately, there are signs that indicate when a person is becoming a problem drinker. Self-recognition requires knowledge of the early signs of alcoholism, the honesty to admit the problem, and the willingness to submit to the only completely sure remedy—to stop drinking.

Anyone who drinks alcoholic beverages should know the early signs of alcoholism and should be on the alert for them as he observes his own behavior. The progress toward alcoholism and the progression of alcoholism is shown in Figure 3.1.

ESCAPE DRINKING

As they become occasional drinkers, many people learn to enjoy the feelings of relief from tension and escape from reality that alcohol can provide. The first step toward alcoholism is taken when a person starts to drink specifically for these effects. About one-fifth of all drinkers fall into the category of *occasional escape drinkers*. These people are not yet alcoholics, but they should be very aware of the possible development of alcoholism. In those who are progressing toward alcoholism, escape drinking becomes more and more frequent. It may quickly develop into a pattern of heavy drinking every night or every weekend.

Another pattern of developing alcoholism which should not be ignored is the "binge" pattern. The binge drinker or periodic alcoholic may go for weeks or months without drinking any alcohol, but then goes

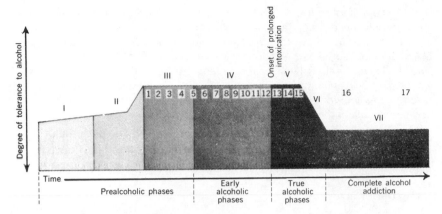

Figure 3.1 *The progression of alcoholism.*

1. Secret drinking. *The alcoholic often sneaks his drinks.*

2. A preoccupation with alcohol. *Before a party an alcoholic is often more interested in what drinks will be served than in who will be the guests.*

3. Gulping the first two drinks. *The alcoholic drinks for effects rather than the taste.*

4. Guilt feelings about drinking. *As an alcoholic, often subconsciously, begins to realize that his drinking habits are not normal, he develops feelings of guilt which lead to: (a) avoiding talking about alcohol, (b) rationalizing his drinking behavior, (c) grandiose behavior, (d) persistent remorse over drinking.*

5. Periods of total abstinence. *He will "go on the wagon" to prove that he can "take it or leave it."*

6. Changing drinking patterns. *In an attempt to drink in a controlled manner, the alcoholic frequently varies his drinking pattern, trying different types of liquor, different mixers, or different times and places in which to drink. He feels that there must be some way to drink without losing control.*

7. Behavior becomes alcohol-centered. *He avoids places and activities that might interfere with his drinking.*

8. Change in habits of family. *The family of an alcoholic may either withdraw into the home for fear of embarrassment or, in contrast, may become very active in outside activities as a means of escape from the home environment.*

9. Unreasonable resentments. *The alcoholic often builds up tremendous resentments and self-pity over some minor or imaginary injustice he has suffered.*

10. Hiding bottles. *The alcoholic often takes elaborate precautions against the possibility of running out of liquor.*

11. Neglect of proper nutrition. *Because the alcoholic has little interest in food, he often suffers from malnutrition.*

12. Decrease in sexual drive. *As a result of his poor physical and emotional condition, the alcoholic may suffer from a decrease in sexual drive. This may lead to "alcoholic jealousy," where he accuses his wife of having relations with other men.*

13. Regular early-day drinking. *This dependence indicates alcohol addiction (Phase V).*

14. Prolonged periods of intoxication. *Each such "bender" lasts until the alcoholic is too sick to continue drinking.*

15. Loss of tolerance. *At this time the alcoholic becomes intoxicated on far less liquor than ever before and stays intoxicated much longer.*

16. Mental impairment. *In the later stages of alcoholism, the thought processes are clouded with or without the presence of alcohol.*

17. Failure of the rationalization system. *Eventually his rationalization system breaks down and he admits defeat. Although he continues to drink, he is now readily accessible to treatment and willing to try anything to regain sobriety. If not, he may die at this stage.*

on a drinking spree that lasts for days or even weeks. The periodic drinker may be just as much an alcoholic as the regular drinker. He is even more likely to lose his job, due to his habit of staying drunk for days at a time.

THE ALCOHOLIC BLACKOUT

An alcoholic blackout is a period of temporary amnesia. It should not be confused with passing out, which involves unconsciousness. *Anyone who drinks too much will pass out.* He will then be unconscious or asleep. Passing out is not a sign of alcoholism; it merely indicates the drinker's poor judgment or lack of experience with alcoholic beverages—or, of course, his desire to reach a state of temporary oblivion.

A blackout is something else entirely. The drinker remains conscious and appears fully aware of what he is doing. He may appear normal to others, and he may seem fully capable of walking, talking, driving, dancing, and drinking as usual. But after he has finished drinking, the drinker who has had a blackout will have no memory of what took place while he drank. He will remember neither the major events nor the minor details. His memory will have blacked out everything that happened after those first few drinks. A blackout usually lasts for several hours; during a binge, however, it may last for several days.

Anyone who has had such a blackout either *is* an alcoholic or *is very nearly so.* Blackouts usually occur first after several months or years of drinking, but some alcoholics report that they have experienced blackouts from the very beginning of their drinking.

LOSS OF CONTROL

The most important symptom of alcoholism is *loss of control* (Figure 3.1). This means that the alcoholic cannot stop at a reasonable number of drinks once he starts drinking but must continue until he is drunk or sick. Depending on the drinking pattern of the individual, his drinking will continue for hours, days, or even weeks.

Loss of control does not mean that the alcoholic cannot choose whether or not he will drink on a certain day. He still has the choice of whether to begin drinking or not. But if he does start to drink, he will not be able to stop. An alcoholic is often heard to brag, "I can take it or leave it alone." This statement is only true in that he can take the first drink or leave it alone.

The person who suffers loss of control is an alcoholic. He may try to fight his loss of control by changing to another type of liquor or another drinking pattern, but these measures will not help. His only hope is to stop drinking entirely. He will probably never be able to return to controlled drinking.

Like blackouts, loss of control usually develops after months or years of drinking, but it may occur even in the beginning drinker. Thus, there is no definite time required for the development of alcoholism. Most cases of alcoholism develop after months or years of controlled drinking, but some people show alcoholic drinking patterns with their very first drink.

PREOCCUPATION WITH ALCOHOL

If alcohol gradually plays an increasingly important role in a person's life and he spends much of his time thinking about drinking or wanting a drink, a serious drinking problem may be developing. When a person with a tendency toward alcoholism looks forward to going to a party, for example, he is more excited about the drinks that will be available than about the companionship and social contacts of the occasion. To the social drinker, on the other hand, the drinks are secondary to other purposes of the party, which may include companionship and communication.

Another danger sign is when a person drinks *more* or *faster* than others at a party. Since the alcoholic or problem drinker is after a quick effect, he "belts" (gulps down) several drinks. He finds he always wants "one more" after others have stopped drinking.

SIGNS OF GUILT

The problem drinker often develops a sense of guilt about his drinking. This may be a conscious feeling, but it is more often subconscious, revealed through certain behavior patterns.

Secret drinking is one sign that a person has guilt feelings about his drinking habits. Sneaking drinks when no one is looking is good evidence that he sees his drinking as abnormal and something to hide. The controlled, nonproblem drinker finds no cause to hide his drinking.

Rationalization of drinking is another good indication of guilt feelings. The alcoholic can always give a reason for his drinking. He says he drinks because his spouse nags him, his children make him nervous, business is poor, business is good, or any one of many other well-worn excuses. All of these are rationalizations. Everyone has problems, but the alcoholic tries to escape his problems through drinking instead of taking action to try to solve them. Any drinker who finds himself offering reasons for his drinking should seriously consider the possibility that he may have a drinking problem. The nonproblem drinker never feels it necessary to give any excuse for wanting a drink.

Advancing Alcoholism

Alcoholism is a progressive behavior problem. Every case of alcoholism progresses at its own speed. Some alcoholics reach an advanced state in just a few months; others take many years to reach the condition shown in Figure 3.1. Oddly, as a general rule, women alcoholics tend to progress to the advanced stages much faster than do men. The following symptoms of advancing alcoholism are arranged in order of expected occurrence; not every individual experiences them in this sequence.

PERIODS OF UNHAPPINESS OR DEPRESSION

Although alcoholics may have a carefree, happy appearance, they are, in reality, usually very unhappy and disturbed. An alcoholic may have periods of remorse during which his guilt feelings come painfully to the surface. He may experience what is commonly called a "crying jag" or "crying drunk" during which he drinks and broods. He may feel sorry for himself or regard himself as a worthless failure. To make himself feel better, he relives his past glories. He brags to others about his achievements, often exaggerating them or telling outright lies. To reinforce his stories, he may throw money around as if he were very wealthy. He even buys drinks for total strangers, spending money he really cannot afford.

The alcoholic often suffers from feelings of persecution. He sees himself as the victim of much injustice inflicted by his spouse, his employer, the police, the law—all of society. He refuses to believe that his drinking has brought on his problems. As he uses this imaginary persecution as an excuse for further drinking, the problems continue to increase. As long as the alcoholic believes that his problems are the result of his persecution by others, the chance of his recovery is poor. Until he realizes that his drinking is the *cause* of his problems, not a remedy, he will not be able to stop drinking.

FINANCIAL PROBLEMS

An alcoholic usually has employment problems. These problems start when he begins to miss mornings or entire days of work. The problems become more serious when he starts to drink or is intoxicated on the job. These actions are grounds for immediate dismissal from almost any job. It is very difficult for the alcoholic to get another job when he has been fired from the last one for drinking; thus he often finds himself unemployed.

Even if employed, he is still likely to have serious financial trouble. Only the wealthiest people can afford the high cost of alcoholism. First, there is the cost of alcoholic beverages, which is especially high if the alcoholic is a bar drinker. The bar drinker may easily spend $15.00 and the home drinker $5.00 per day for drinks. It is not unusual for an alcoholic to consume at least a fifth of a gallon of liquor per day. In addition to the cost of his own drinks, the alcoholic may spend money buying drinks for others he meets in bars. He also tends to waste money by making unwise purchases while he is intoxicated.

The alcoholic often turns to gambling in an attempt to solve his financial problems. But far more often than not, gambling only leads to further loss of money. Thousands of alcoholics have been caught stealing or embezzling to cover gambling debts or to buy more liquor.

EFFECTS ON MARRIAGE

Many of alcoholism's effects on marriage are the results of the financial problems just described. Money problems always place a strain on a marriage, but when these problems are the direct result of the excessive drinking of one spouse, the other spouse is likely to be highly resentful.

Other problems in the alcoholic's marriage result from the family's loss of his companionship and, in some cases, the maltreatment of family members while he is under the effects of alcohol.

The alcoholic's family tends to become socially isolated. They no longer bring home friends because they fear embarrassment by the alcoholic's actions. This fear is an especially painful problem for the children of an alcoholic mother. They know that she is likely to be at home and intoxicated at any time of the day or evening.

Another problem in the alcoholic's marriage is jealousy. The alcoholic often suffers a loss of sexual drive. As the sexual relationship in the marriage deteriorates and intercourse becomes less frequent, the alcoholic tends to blame this deterioration on anything but the real cause—alcohol-induced reduction of sexual drive. Very often, the alcoholic's spouse is then accused of having extramarital love affairs. An atmosphere of suspicion and jealousy may develop which can lead to the eventual end of the marriage.

TRUE ALCOHOL ADDICTION—REGULAR MORNING DRINKING

Alcohol is an addictive substance. After years of heavy drinking, the alcoholic may require the constant presence of alcohol in his body to prevent withdrawal symptoms. He must now start his day with a drink, commonly called the "eye-opener." He may drink it from a bottle placed next to his bed the night before, or he may become a regular patron of bars that advertise Open 6 AM (Figure 3.2).

If the fully addicted alcoholic is deprived of alcohol, his first withdrawal symptoms are usually shaking of the hands, arms, and body. His mood will be apprehensive, fearful, and irritable; he may have frightening hallucinations. Once such a complete addiction is established, the alcoholic should *not* be forced to sober up without medical care, as there is a chance he will go into convulsions and perhaps even die.

Figure 3.2 *Open 6 AM. This sign is typical of bars catering to early-morning drinkers.*

MENTAL CHANGES IN LATE ALCOHOLISM

Many alcoholics eventually suffer a drastic disintegration of personality. If they do not stop drinking as soon as the first signs of such changes appear, their minds may be permanently damaged. It is believed that much of this brain damage is due to the combined effects of severe thiamine deficiency and alcohol.

A type of psychosis that commonly appears and recurs frequently in late alcoholics is *Alcohol-Barbiturate Abstinence Syndrome* or *delirium tremens,* commonly called "the D.T.s." An attack of D.T.s lasts from 2 to 10 days and may be brought on by injury, illness, or withdrawal from alcohol. The symptoms include confusion and violent, vivid visual hallucinations. The alcoholic will be fearful and apprehensive, restless and sleepless. He may have convulsions resembling epileptic seizures. After several days, the attack will end and the alcoholic will sleep deeply for a period.

After several attacks of delirium tremens, a very serious condition called "wet brain" may develop. This is a chronic, or long-term, condition, seldom curable and often fatal. The alcoholic's thought processes are completely disrupted. All functions of his nervous system are impaired. The alcoholic who reaches this stage will either die or spend the rest of his life in an institution.

Psychological Causes of Drug Abuse

In humans, adjustment to living is much more complicated than in simpler animals. We have the ability to reason and make decisions based upon learned behavior, physiological needs, and emotional needs. Why do we do things we do? Why do we feel the way we do? The answers to these questions come largely from our understanding of and reaction to how basic human needs are fulfilled and how the frustrations of unfulfilled needs are met.

The most basic of human needs are the *physiological needs,* such as those for food, water, sleep, and sexual satisfaction. The compulsive drug user, addict, and alcoholic substitutes the substance he is abusing for the objects of his physiological needs. He eats only the food and water needed to keep alive. The decrease in sexual drive in addicts and alcoholics is well documented.

Curiosity or the *need to know and understand* is often the major reason for first drug experimentations—too often, with only street knowledge ("I know because I have tried it") of drug effects. Since no two people are exactly alike, such knowledge can produce either the thrills a curious young person is looking for in an extremely structured society, or death.

The *need for love and belonging* is very important. Young people feel a strong need for friends, companionship, and acceptance by a group. Group acceptance through drug use may cause an individual to progress from experimentation to being an occasional user and then a regular or compulsive member of the drug subculture. Opportunities for belonging to a group without using drugs can also help one to remain or become uninvolved with drugs. Such group belonging is the basis of therapeutic communities and organizations like Alcoholics Anonymous.

Every person needs *self-esteem*—a feeling of personal value or worth. The opposite of self-esteem is feelings of dependence, inferiority, weakness, helplessness, and despair. Such feelings are common as both the cause and outcome of compulsive drug abuse. Self-esteem is one of the hardest needs to satisfy in a drug abuser, and the frustration of this need keeps putting him back "on the street." One way to break the drug abuse cycle is to give the user duties or jobs that he can perform well, bringing sincere praise and building self-esteem.

To an addict, Utopia is an unlimited supply of drugs: "If I were guaranteed drugs for the rest of my life, I would never want anything else." This is not so, but when this need is satisfied, as in methadone maintenance therapy, the emotional needs (love and belonging, self-esteem) emerge and can be dealt with through the many forms of psychotherapy.

Emotional Maturity and Drug Abuse

PERSONALITY

Personality can be divided into three areas: (1) personal pleasure and gratification, (2) mature, appropriate behavior, (3) self-ideal and personal judgment of right and wrong. Maturity acts as a regulator between the need for pleasure and satisfaction and the demands of conscience (personal judgment of acceptable behavior). An individual matures as he learns to respond to the emotional, social, and environmental pressures around him and still attain satisfaction and pleasure.

Aggression is seen by many authorities as a basic, childish means of obtaining pleasure. Young children enjoy being aggressive. As someone matures aggression can be expressed in both harmful and beneficial ways. Drug abuse is a self-inflicted form of aggression, especially when someone is injecting drugs and needs the needle itself for full enjoyment. Competition, in business, politics, and sports, is seen as acceptable expression of basic human aggression.

The need for pleasure in hedonistic personalities, regardless of the physical, social, or legal consequences, is immature. The release of aggression or the extreme pleasure many find with drugs also shows a lack of emotional maturity. Regular and compulsive drug abusers cannot control their behavior adequately and operate at a "child role" level of maturity. This inability to maintain normal emotional control is commonly called "emotional or mental illness."

EMOTIONAL ILLNESS

Emotionally ill drug abusers experience an abnormal amount of tension and show it through nervousness. The occasional drug user or social drinker starts to establish an emotionally ill pattern of using drugs either to block out tensions or to provide experiences that make the tensions seem insignificant. When not under the influence of drugs, he becomes increasingly alert (hyperalert)—sounds are exaggerated, lights look more intense, perception seems keener. He looks for possible dangers, refuses to relax during sleep, displays restlessness (walking the floor or driving aimlessly about in his car). He shows increased touchiness, tearfulness, irritability, nervous laughter, moodiness, or depression. He may worry obsessively and daydream excessively. All such behavior impairs realistic thinking and effective action, and the individual begins to be overzealous in identifying with some cause—often the right to use drugs. By this time the drug abuser has moved from being an occasional user to a regular user.

The regular drug user, periodic alcoholic, compulsive drug abuser, addict, or chronic alcoholic makes drug use a permanent part of his personality and is mentally ill while under the influence of drugs. Such an individual abuses drugs or alcohol as a means of coping with the stresses of his environment. During prolonged periods between drug use (when "straight" or "on the wagon") he is normal and functions within society. But when stresses are placed upon him he cannot find any other means of control; he turns to drugs or alcohol and the changes in personality are often very dramatic. This is why this behavior is termed a "personality deformity," "personality disorder," having an "addictive personality."

Periodically the individual will dip deeper into mental illness, showing open aggression or the symptoms of a classical mental disorder. Such dips have occurred in the alcoholic who beats or abuses members of the family, the drunk who can always find a fight, and the extreme psychotic states produced by hallucinogenic drugs, especially LSD and mescaline.

In light of the millions of Americans who are addicted to alcohol or narcotics or who chronically abuse other drugs, drug abuse represents the largest single symptom of mental illness in the United States.

Sociological Causes of Drug Abuse

Before an individual ever comes into contact with drugs, he often has an attitude either for or against their use. This attitude, in general, corresponds to that of his friends and social group, his neighborhood, or the general community in which he lives. In areas where the use of drugs is discouraged, both the availability and the abuse of drugs is low.

Equally crucial to the person's continued use of drugs, after experimentation, is the reaction of his social group to his initial experience: approval or disapproval, reward or punishment, praise or ridicule. If he decides to continue, two consequences are inevitable: (1) He will become progressively disillusioned with values and standards of non-drug users and will begin to feel abused and misunderstood under their standards. (2) His identification and ties with the drug world will increase.

Advance knowledge of both the properties of drugs and the social reactions to their abuse can influence the course of an individual's use of drugs. Although an individual may be addicted, if he does not know about dependence and withdrawal symptoms and no one points these out to him as evidences of addiction (as in the cases of millions of persons addicted to alcohol), he may never actually admit to himself that he is an addict. Even a person with a mature personality needs strong social pressures or adult guidance to reverse the course of drug abuse after he has established a drug dependence.

The abnormal social behavior of drug-influenced individuals is an increasingly prominent sociological, medical, and legal problem. This problem actually involves personal responsibility for an individual's behavior during times of drug-induced behavioral changes, mood modifications, or personality illnesses. Prohibition of drugs is not the answer. The proper control of drug abuse lies in solving nine problems among the people who use drugs, outlined by Helen N. Nowlis, Professor of Psychology, University of Rochester:

1. *Ignorance*—about the actions of chemical substances upon the complex, delicately balanced chemical system that is the living person. There is also a lack of knowledge about causes of variations in human behavior. Here drug abuse is a problem of opinion, attitude, and belief in the absence of knowledge.

2. *Semantics*—talking, thinking, acting rationally in an area in which every term is entangled in myth, emotions, assumptions, beliefs, and attitudes that too often turn the dialogue into a futile argument.

3. *Communications*—among and between many. Scientists in different areas often lack communication among themselves. These individuals are also largely unable to communicate their ideas and findings to laymen. Also, there is a communication problem between the generations brought up before and during the development of automation, television, jet travel, nuclear energy (and the hydrogen bomb), large urban centers, cramped schools, and an affluent social order, and a generation which has known no other conditions.

4. *Lack of understanding of scientific method and concepts*—that there are no simple relationships between cause and effect in human behavior. Human behavior has many facets, and there is a difference between correlation and causation. The design and execution of experiments may be open to bias, and a consequent "conclusion" based on one experiment has no meaning except in terms of a large number of dimensions. Statements about these results, even at a biologic level, are in terms of averages and probabilities.

5. *Living, learning, and growing*—change is always taking place and the future is increasingly unpredictable.

6. *Philosophy of social control*—in a complex society the individual's relationship to social values is expressed in law. When these laws impinge upon an individual they react directly to the law.

7. *Education*—its relationship to current social values. This becomes a problem of the relationship of the institution to the needs of society.

8. A *"pill society"*—a chemical solution for any problem of unpleasantness and discomfort. This "pill society" spends more on alcohol, tranquilizers, and sleeping pills than it does on education or the social and economic ills of the nation.

9. *Increasing retreat in the face of complex difficult problems*—the biggest "cop out" of all time. Many insist that everything is all good or all bad and define good as "not bad" and bad as "not good."

Interactions of Causes

Although initial drug experimentation and selection of a specific drug (heroin, marijuana, alcohol) is generally dictated by social factors such as availability, friends, and social environment, individuals tend to obtain experiences from drugs related to their own basic needs. Psychological processes can override physical drug effects. Ultimately, an individual experiments until he finds a drug whose physical properties produce the state of consciousness that fills his emotional needs. For example, the individual whose first experiences with LSD produce an amphetaminelike effect tends eventually to turn to amphetamines, which fill his needs more efficiently.

Emotional factors become more important in drug abuse and social factors less important as use becomes heavier and more compulsive. For instance, depressant drugs remove an individual from the stresses and anxieties of society. Heroin does this very quickly; alcohol, slowly but for a longer period of time. Hallucinogenic drugs can compensate for a lack of experiences, control emotions, or help someone deal with aggressions, while amphetamines help increase output of physical energy.

There is no single reason for abusing drugs, no single pattern of abuse, and no inevitable outcome. Drug abusers are individuals and are susceptible to many factors that are responsible not only for chronic use but also for relapses. A person desperately trying to stop using drugs must progressively fulfill his emotional and social needs to resume control of his life.

Summary

I. Drug abuse behavior

    A. All individuals introduced to drugs will fall within one or more of the following categories of drug behavior

    B. Categories of drug abusers

        1. Experimenters—individuals who have tried drugs and have no intention of using illegal drugs again

        2. Occasional users—individuals who find they need and enjoy the social, personal, and emotional gratification that mood-modifying drugs give them

        3. Regular users—individuals who use drugs one or more times per week

        4. Compulsive drug abusers (addicts or alcoholics)—use drugs as their means of coping with the stress of the environment

II. What is alcoholism? What is an alcoholic?

    A. Alcoholism is a chronic behavioral disorder manifested in the alcoholic

    B. An alcoholic is someone whose drinking interferes with a useful life

III. Early signs of alcoholism

    A. Escape drinking: this first step occurs when a person starts to drink specifically for the effects of alcohol on the body

    B. The alcoholic blackout

        1. A period of temporary amnesia

        2. While in a blackout an individual remains conscious and seems fully aware of what he is doing, but he will have no recollection of what took place while he drank

    C. Loss of control

        1. The most important symptom of alcoholism

        2. The alcoholic cannot stop at a reasonable number of drinks once he starts drinking and must continue until he is drunk or sick

        3. The person who suffers loss of control is an alcoholic

D. Preoccupation with alcohol

    1. The person with a tendency toward alcoholism spends much of his time thinking about drinking or wanting a drink
    2. He often "belts" or gulps his drink down
    3. He finds he always wants "one more" after others have stopped drinking

E. Signs of guilt

    1. The problem drinker often develops a sense of guilt about the amount he is drinking
    2. Secret drinking is one sign that a person has guilt feelings about his drinking habits
    3. *Rationalization* of drinking behavior is another good indication of guilt feelings

IV. Advancing alcoholism

    A. Periods of unhappiness or depression
        1. Alcoholics are usually very unhappy
        2. To make himself feel better, he relives his past glories
        3. The alcoholic often suffers from feelings of persecution

    B. Until he realizes that his drinking is the cause of his problems, the problems continue to increase
    C. Financial problems

        1. Alcoholics usually have employment problems
        2. Even if they are employed, they are still likely to have serious financial trouble because of their expensive habit

    D. Effects on marriage

        1. Many of the effects on a marriage are results of the financial problems just described
        2. The alcoholic's family tends to become socially isolated
        3. Jealousy—the loss of sexual drive in the alcoholic often leads tc the alcoholic accusing the spouse of having extramarital love affairs

    E. True alcohol addiction—regular morning drinking. The fully addicted alcoholic if deprived of alcohol will manifest all of the symptoms of withdrawal

    F. Mental changes in late alcoholism

        1. Many alcoholics eventually suffer a drastic disintegration of personality
        2. The alcoholic's thought processes become completely disrupted
        3. All functions of the nervous system are impaired
        4. The alcoholic that reaches this stage will either die or spend the rest of his life in an institution

V. Psychological causes of drug abuse behavior

    A. Humans have the ability to reason and make decisions based upon learned behavior and physiological and emotional needs
    B. Cause of drug use is based upon one's understanding and reactions to basic human needs

1. Curiosity, or the need to know and understand, is often the major reason for first drug experimentations

2. Need for love and belonging (acceptance by a group) may cause an individual to progress from drug experimentation to becoming an occasional user, then to becoming a regular or compulsive user

3. Lack of self-esteem—a feeling of personal value or worth—produces feelings of dependence, inferiority, weakness, helplessness, and despair. Such feelings are common as both cause and outcome of compulsive drug abuse

4. The compulsive drug user substitutes drugs for his physiological needs such as food, sleep, and sexual satisfaction

C. Emotional maturity and drug abuse

1. Maturity of an individual acts as a regulator between the need for pleasure and satisfaction and personal judgment of acceptable behavior

2. Drug abusers exhibit various levels of emotional illness

a. Experimenters exhibit more than normal amounts of tension and "nervousness"

b. Occasional drug users and social drinkers start to establish emotionally sick patterns by using drugs to either "block out tension" or provide experiences

c. Regular drug users, periodic alcoholics, and compulsive drug abusers make drug use a permanent part of their personalities

VI. Sociological causes of drug abuse behavior

A. Before ever coming into contact with drugs an individual usually has an attitude either for or against drug use

B. Crucial to a person's continued use of drugs is the approval or disapproval of his social group

C. Abnormal social behavior of drug-influenced individuals is an increasingly prominent sociological, medical, and legal problem

D. The real problem is not drugs but the people who use drugs

VII. Interactions of factors

A. Social factors, psychological processes, physical properties of a drug, and emotional factors are all important in drug abuse

B. There is no single pattern of inevitable outcomes when drugs are abused

Questions for Review

1. Not all individuals introduced to drugs will abuse them. What are the categories of drug abusers?

2. What is alcoholism?

3. Causes of drug use are based upon one's understanding and reactions to basic human needs. Discuss how these needs are fulfilled by drug use. Discuss how these same needs may be used to treat someone for drug use.

4. Explain the statement that "compulsive drug users are mentally ill."

Chapter 4
ALCOHOL ABUSE

Alcohol is a socially acceptable mood-modifying substance. The only distinction between alcohol and the drugs discussed in the previous chapter is that moderate use of alcohol is legally and socially acceptable by the majority of Americans. About 70 percent of the adults in the United States make at least some use of alcohol. Yet alcohol has a potential for abuse greater than many of the drugs previously discussed.

Alcohol is a sedative, the most widely used and abused mood-modifying sedative in the United States. The average person has a much greater chance of becoming addicted to alcohol, because of its legal availability, than any other mood-modifying drug.

The more you learn about the nature and effects of alcoholic beverages, the more likely you will be able to make intelligent decisions about their use. Your friends are not a reliable source for facts about alcohol. Even people who drink regularly may know very little about alcohol and how it works.

Alcoholic Beverages

Kinds of Alcohol

Among the many varieties of alcohol is *methyl alcohol,* commonly called "wood alcohol," which is used in many commercial products such as antifreezes and fuels. It must never be consumed, since even small amounts can cause blindness and death. "Bootleg" liquor (liquor sold illegally to avoid payment of taxes) is occasionally found to contain wood alcohol and therefore should never be consumed.

A second common type of alcohol—also poisonous—is *isopropyl alcohol*. While it is usually called "rubbing alcohol," it is also used as a disinfectant and a solvent.

The only kind of alcohol that can be consumed safely in alcoholic drinks is *ethyl alcohol,* or "grain alcohol." "Denatured" alcohol is ethyl alcohol to which poisonous chemicals have been added. The removal of these poisons requires complex laboratory procedures, so there is no household way to make denatured alcohol safe for drinking. Ethyl alcohol is produced from the fermentation of sugar by yeasts. Each type of alcoholic beverage is produced from a specific source of sugar. Beer, for example, is made from fermented malted (sprouted) barley. Wine is fermented grape juice. The "hard" liquors are made from the distilled products of the fermentation of various grains and other sugar sources (see Table 4.1). Because distillation greatly concentrates the alcoholic content of a beverage, the distilled liquors are much stronger than beer or wine and are often made into highballs, i.e., diluted with water or soft drinks.

TABLE 4.1 Source and Alcoholic Content of Alcoholic Beverages

Beverage	Source	Distilled	Percent of Alcohol by Volume
Beer	Malted barley	No	4–6
Ale	Malted barley	No	6–8
Wine	Grape juice	No	12–21
Whiskey	Malted grains	Yes	40–50
Brandy	Grape juice	Yes	40–50
Rum	Molasses	Yes	40–50
Vodka	Various sources	Yes	40–50
Gin	Various sources	Yes	40–50

The alcoholic content of alcoholic beverages is expressed as "proof," a figure which is exactly double the alcoholic percentage. Thus 86 proof whiskey is 43 percent alcohol. The alcoholic content of wine is usually expressed directly as a percentage (see Table 4.2).

Food Values of Alcoholic Beverages

In addition to alcohol and water, alcoholic beverages contain mainly flavoring and coloring agents. They have almost no food value. As shown in Table 4.3, there are no vitamins, minerals, fats, proteins, or usable carbohydrates in most alcoholic beverages. The one exception is beer, and the amounts of nutrients present are insignificant.

TABLE 4.2 Amounts of Alcoholic Beverages Containing Similar Quantities of Alcohol

Beverage		Alcohol Content %	Amount of Beverage Giving ½ Oz. of Alcohol (in Ounces)
Beer		4	12
Dinner wine		12	4
Dessert wine		21	2½
Distilled liquor	80 proof	40	1¼
Distilled liquor	100 proof	50	1

TABLE 4.3 Nutritional Values of Alcoholic Beverages

Food Nutrient	Type of Beverage and Quantity		
	Beer (12 ounces)	Whiskey (2 ounces)	Wine (8 ounces)
Calories	171.0	140.0	275.0
Calories from alcohol	114.0	140.0	240.0
Protein (grams)	2.0	0.0	0.0
Fat (grams)	0.0	0.0	0.0
Carbohydrate (grams)	12.0	0.0	8.5
Thiamine (milligrams)	0.1	0.0	0.0
Nicotinic acid (milligrams)	0.75	0.0	0.0
Riboflavin (milligrams)	10.0	0.0	0.0
Ascorbic acid (milligrams)	0.0	0.0	0.0
Folic acid (milligrams)	0.0	0.0	0.0

Calories, however, are abundant in alcoholic beverages. There are 7 calories per gram in pure alcohol, nearly as many as in pure fat or oil (9 calories per gram). But, alcohol calories are not in a form that can be used directly by the body. Therefore alcoholic beverages are classified as an incomplete food and the calories are called "empty" calories.

Effects of Alcohol on the Brain

From the standpoint of explaining why people drink, the most significant effect of alcohol can be seen if we examine how it affects the brain and central nervous system.

Alcohol is a sedative, or depressant; in other words, it slows down the action of the brain. With small amounts of alcohol in the blood, the first part of the brain to be depressed is the center that controls judgment and inhibitions, often called the "highest" center of the brain. When this part of the brain is depressed, a person feels an apparent stimulation due to his release from inhibitions.

As the drinker takes in more alcohol, more primitive, or "lower," parts of the brain are depressed progressively. If extremely high levels of alcohol are in the blood, the primitive reflex centers that control breathing and other body functions may be depressed to the point that the person dies. Such high blood-alcohol levels are seldom reached through normal drinking, however, because a person usually vomits or becomes unconscious first. Nevertheless, a fatal dose of alcohol could be consumed if a person very rapidly drank a large quantity of straight distilled liquor.

Effects on Sensory Perception and Coordination

Sight is the first sense affected by alcohol. Although small amounts of alcohol increase a person's sensitivity to light, he is less able to distinguish between two different intensities of light, and focusing becomes more difficult. Increasing amounts of alcohol cause a great loss of vision. Hearing is affected less than sight, but is still significantly impaired at higher blood-alcohol levels. The other senses definitely impaired by alcohol are equilibrium, taste, smell, and touch.

Because all the voluntary muscles are under the control of the brain and nervous system, muscle control is impaired at all blood-alcohol levels. This results in loss of coordination and lengthened reaction time. These changes are especially detrimental to automobile drivers. Some people feel that their driving ability is improved by small amounts of alcohol, but the truth is that alcohol only makes these people *think* they are driving better. Half of the 55,000 deaths on the highway each year and half of the million major injuries suffered in auto accidents are caused by an individual "under the influence of alcohol." While the blood-alcohol level required for a drunk-driving conviction ranges from .10 to .15 percent, experiments have repeatedly shown that driving ability is severely impaired at a .10 percent blood-alcohol level. In a young person or someone not familiar with how alcohol affects the body, alcohol is a factor in accidents at blood-alcohol levels as low as .03 percent. Michigan, in the first year following its lowering of the drinking age from 21 to 18, reported a 141 percent increase in arrests for drunk driving in this age group.

The close relationship between drinking and traffic accidents is so well known that one might wonder why people still insist on driving after drinking. Unfortunately, the intoxicated person usually does not realize how badly his driving ability has been impaired. The same effects on the brain that make him a dangerous driver also make him unable to realize how poor his driving ability has become.

The person who drinks must plan ahead, when he is still sober, to have other transportation available for his ride home. Better yet, he should limit his drinking to no more than *one drink per hour* and to a *total of no more than 4 beers or 4 ounces of distilled liquor in one day or evening.* By limiting his drinking, he can reduce both the risk he takes in driving and the total problem of alcohol abuse as well.

Half of all murders in the United States can be linked to the drinking of alcoholic beverages. Either the killer, the victim, or both had been drinking at the time of the crime. Twenty-five percent of the suicide victims have significant amounts of alcohol in their blood when found. Blood-alcohol concentrations resulting from different amounts of alcohol are shown in Table 4.4.

Even with all of this, parents seem relatively unconcerned about young people drinking alcohol. Police often hear: "Oh, he was *just* drinking —Thank God! he's not on drugs."

Judgment and Self-Control

Like several of the drugs discussed in Chapter 2, alcohol can temporarily produce a state of euphoria. The desire to achieve this state is one of the main reasons that people drink. Most people become more careless when drinking than they normally would be, and they do things they ordinarily would not do. They say things that their good judgment would ordinarily keep them from saying and often feel that what they are saying is especially witty or profound. It should be stressed that this loss of judgment occurs at rather low blood-alcohol levels. The light drinker's driving ability is reduced more by his impaired judgment than by his loss of muscle control.

Alcohol so greatly impairs the muscle control of heavy drinkers that they find simple tasks difficult and moderately difficult tasks impossible.

Memory and Learning Ability

Alcohol interferes with both the storage and retrieval of information. When a person is under the influence of alcohol, his ability to learn and to recall past events and information is decreased. His problem-solving ability is also greatly diminished. Even simple puzzles and arithmetic problems may be difficult or impossible for the intoxicated person to solve.

Effects of Alcohol on the Other Body Organs

The functioning of almost every part of the body can be affected by alcohol. Some organs are influenced by even small amounts of alcohol; other organs or systems respond only to high blood-alcohol levels. But most of the effects associated with moderate drinking are due to the alcohol's influence on the brain rather than to its direct influence on the other organs.

Digestive System

Moderate drinkers sometimes notice a slight improvement in their digestion when they consume wine with a meal or drink a cocktail before dinner. This improvement is the result of two effects of alcohol on the body. One effect is the stimulation of the production of stomach acids. The second, probably more important, action is the relaxing or sedative effect alcohol has on the nervous system; poor digestion is often the result of nervous tension.

Alcohol may damage the stomach of the heavy drinker. High concentrations of alcohol are definitely irritating to the stomach lining and may lead to chronic gastritis. The irritating effect of alcohol on the stomach lining is also the reason that persons who drink too much may vomit. Vomiting is a reflex action that relieves the stomach of any irritating substance.

Liver

Liver ailments are especially common among alcoholics. About 75 percent of all alcoholics show some degree of loss of liver function. About 8 percent of all alcoholics eventually develop the often fatal cirrhosis (hardening) of the liver. Cirrhosis is six times as common among alcoholics as among the general population.

The liver is important in eliminating alcohol from the body. After drinking, a person eliminates small amounts of alcohol in his sweat, breath, and urine. But over 90 percent of the alcohol he consumes is oxidized (broken down) to form carbon dioxide and water. This oxidation process has several steps, the first of which occurs only in the liver. The remaining steps take place rapidly in various parts of the body, but since the alcohol must be acted on first by the liver, it is the liver's ability to function that determines the rate at which one "sobers up."

Every individual has a set rate at which he can oxidize alcohol. This rate varies among different people, but it is generally constant for the same person. Blood-alcohol levels, moreover, do not affect the rate of oxidation; it is the same whether an individual has drunk a little alcohol or a lot. In one hour the average person can oxidize the amount of alcohol contained in 6 to 12 ounces of beer, 2 to 4 ounces of wine, or one-half to one ounce of distilled liquor. No method has been found to increase this rate of oxidation significantly. Some people try vigorous exercise, drinking strong coffee, or breathing pure oxygen, but these measures have little effect in an attempt to sober up.

Proper Use of Alcohol

Some people argue that any consumption of alcoholic beverages is improper. But the majority of Americans find no medical, moral, legal, or religious reason for not making moderate use of alcoholic beverages. We therefore offer some suggestions that may help a person avoid problems in drinking.

Even those people who fully approve of drinking and themselves drink regularly usually disapprove of certain types of drinking behavior, for

TABLE 4.4 Blood Alcohol Levels (Percent Alcohol in Blood)

Body Weight (Lb.)	Drinks[a]											
	1	2	3	4	5	6	7	8	9	10	11	12
100	.038	.075	.113	.150	.188	.225	.263	.300	.338	.375	.413	.450
120	.031	.063	.094	.125	.156	.188	.219	.250	.281	.313	.344	.375
140	.027	.054	.080	.107	.134	.161	.188	.214	.241	.268	.295	.321
160	.023	.047	.070	.094	.117	.141	.164	.188	.211	.234	.258	.281
180	.021	.042	.063	.083	.104	.125	.146	.167	.188	.208	.229	.250
200	.019	.038	.056	.075	.094	.113	.131	.150	.169	.188	.206	.225
220	.017	.034	.051	.068	.085	.102	.119	.136	.153	.170	.188	.205
240	.016	.031	.047	.063	.078	.094	.109	.125	.141	.156	.172	.188

Under .05	.05 to .10	.10 to .15	Over .15
Driving is not seriously impaired.	Driving becomes increasingly dangerous. .08 legally drunk in Utah.	Driving is dangerous. Legally drunk in most states.	Driving is very dangerous. Legally drunk in any state.

[a] One drink equals one ounce of 100 proof liquor or 12 ounces of beer.
Source: Reprinted through the courtesy of the New Jersey Department of Law and Public Safety, Division of Motor Vehicles, Trenton, New Jersey.

example, drunken driving or such antisocial behavior as physical or verbal violence. Almost all those who approve of drinking do feel that there are times and places where drinking is not appropriate. Any time that a person needs his fullest mental faculties, such as when he is driving or flying or operating machinery, is obviously a poor time to drink. For many employers, drinking or being drunk on the job is grounds for immediate dismissal.

It is very poor policy to drink for courage, for example, in preparation for a job interview or sales conference. This is using alcohol as a crutch and is a step in the direction of alcoholism.

There is, of course, no set answer for the question of how much to drink. While drinking is acceptable in American society, getting drunk is definitely frowned upon. The person who drinks is expected to drink in moderation, without serious impairment of his physical or mental functions.

The social drinker learns to drink slowly and to pace his drinking so that he does not build up a high blood-alcohol level. If a person who can oxidize the alcohol from one drink each hour spaces 4 drinks over the span of a 4-hour party, he will not reach an excessively high blood-alcohol level.

The host or hostess of a party at which drinks are served should feel a certain responsibility for the amount of alcohol the guests drink. He must ask himself how he would feel if someone were involved in a fatal accident on the way home from his party. There should be nonalcoholic drinks available for those who prefer them, and the person who prefers not to drink should not be pressured or ridiculed. No pressure should be put on any guest to drink more than he wants. If he wants to stop at one drink, he should be allowed to. During the last hour or so of a party, coffee should be served. This serves several purposes. Coffee does not counteract alcohol, but the *caffeine* may help overcome the drowsiness that can be as much a cause of accidents as intoxication. The time spent drinking coffee serves as a sobering-up period as well. Finally, the serving of coffee is accepted by most guests as a signal that the party is about over so the host can bring a party to a close when he wishes to. Anyone who is obviously in no condition to drive home should be strongly encouraged to stay overnight, take a taxi, share a ride, or do something other than drive.

Summary

I. Alcoholic beverages

    A. There are many varieties of alcohol

        1. One is *methyl alcohol,* commonly called "wood alcohol"
        2. The second is *isopropyl alcohol,* commonly called "rubbing alcohol"
        3. The only kind of alcohol that can be consumed safely in alcoholic drinks is *ethyl alcohol,* or "grain alcohol"

B. Food values of alcoholic beverages

> **1.** Alcoholic beverages have almost no food value—see Table 3.3
> **2.** However calories are abundant—pure alcohol is 7 calories per gram

II. Effects of alcohol on the brain

A. Alcohol is a sedative and depressant—it slows down the action of the brain

B. Effects on sensory perception and coordination

> **1.** Sight is impaired
> **2.** Hearing is affected, but, to a lesser extent than sight
> **3.** Other senses definitely impaired by alcohol are:
>> **a.** Equilibrium
>> **b.** Taste
>> **c.** Smell
>> **d.** Touch

C. Judgment and self-control

> **1.** Alcohol can temporarily produce a state of euphoria
> **2.** The desire to achieve euphoria is one of the main reasons that people drink
> **3.** The euphoria results in a carelessness that precludes judgment and self-control
> **4.** This impairment of judgment occurs at rather low blood-alcohol levels

D. Memory and Learning Ability. Alcohol interferes with both the storage and retrieval of information from memory

III. Effects of alcohol on the other body organs

A. Most of the effects associated with moderate drinking are due to the alcohol's influence on the brain rather than to its direct effects on the other body organs

B. Digestive System

> **1.** For moderate drinkers, there may be a slight improvement in the digestion
> **2.** But alcohol may also damage the stomach of the heavy drinker

C. Liver

> **1.** Liver ailments are especially common among alcoholics
> **2.** The liver is important in eliminating alcohol from the body

IV. Proper use of alcoholic beverages

A. Majority of Americans find no medical, moral, legal, or religious reasons for not making moderate use of alcoholic beverages

1. Even those who approve of drinking disapprove of certain types of drinking behavior
2. There are times and places where drinking is not appropriate

B. The moderate drinker learns to drink slowly and to pace his drinking so that he does not build up a high blood-alcohol level
C. The host or hostess of a party at which drinks are served should feel a certain responsibility for the amount of alcohol the guests drink

Questions for Review

1. What are the common types of alcohol? In what ways is alcohol used?

2. Proof is a term associated with alcoholic beverages. What does it mean?

3. Alcohol is classified as an incomplete food. Why?

4. Is alcohol a drug? What is its effect on the body?

5. Which part of the brain is first affected by alcohol? What is the significance of this?

6. Does an individual's body weight make a difference in this blood-alcohol level? What factors influence blood-alcohol content?

7. What are hard liquors? What makes them different from other alcoholic beverages?

8. Drug users very often put down those who drink. Do you think there are basic differences between people who use drugs and people who drink alcohol? Between drug abusers and alcohol abusers? Between drugs and alcohol?

9. Do you think the drinking age in your state should be lowered? Why?

Chapter 5

TOBACCO ABUSE

Cigarette smoking has become extremely common in our culture. It is by far the commonest form of drug abuse in the United States today, involving nearly 70 million Americans; however, this has not always been the case. The cigarette consumption of Americans has increased tremendously since the turn of the century. In 1900 the per person (both nonsmokers and smokers 15 years of age and over) consumption rate was less than 50 cigarettes a year. By 1910 this had risen to 138 cigarettes per person per year, to 1,365 cigarettes per person per year in 1930, to 1,828 in 1940, to 3,322 in 1950, 3,888 in 1960, and to over 4,000 cigarettes consumed per person per year in 1967. Reports from the Internal Revenue Bureau (statistics from cigarette sales taxes) show that in late 1967 and early 1968 a reduction began in the per person consumption of cigarettes. As shown in Figure 5.1, this trend continued through early 1971, chiefly owing to older individuals breaking the habit. By 1972 the smoking consumption trend had once again reversed and started upward. The increase mainly reflects a trend of young people (between 15 and 24 years of age) starting to smoke for the first time.

The dependence-producing potential of tobacco is greater than that of alcohol. Most smokers are dependent, regular users, whereas the majority of people are able to use alcohol as social drinkers, intermittently and sensibly. Some individuals begin experimenting with cigarettes as early as 9 or 10 years of age, but most habitual smokers begin somewhere between 15 and 24. Seventy percent of 15-year-old smokers will continue smoking for the next 40 years. Only about 15 percent of smokers are able to

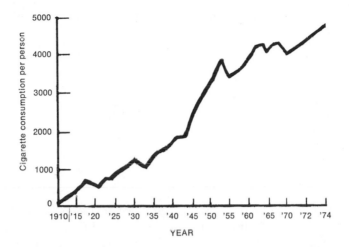

Figure 5.1 *A profile of the growth of cigarette consumption in the United States between 1910 and 1974. These figures include nonsmokers and smokers 15 years old and over. Compiled from United States Department of Agriculture, Economic Research Service Publications.*

stop before the age of 60. Seventy-seven percent of adult smokers have tried to quit or want to quit—few succeed.

Most younger individuals begin smoking because of their friends' smoking behavior. Young adults begin during military service or as a result of the freedom and pressures of the first years of college. Servicemen are introduced to smoking as a "tension reliever." Only in recent years have free gift cigarettes been removed from military hospitals. Tobacco companies also promote their brands to young adults by giving away millions of free cigarettes on or near most college campuses.

Composition and Effects of Tobacco Smoke

Tobacco contains more than a hundred known chemical compounds. Some of the substances found in tobacco remain in the ashes of a burned cigarette; others are greatly changed during the burning process. Moreover, additional compounds are produced during combustion, and it is some of these materials that are of great concern to scientists and physicians. The composition of the cigarette smoke that enters the human body has been the primary aim of most analytical studies.

More than 270 chemical compounds have been identified in cigarette smoke. These include nicotine and at least 15 chemicals known as *carcinogens*—materials which have been proven to cause cancer, either in animal experiments or in observations of humans exposed to them. Table 5.1 lists some of the carcinogens found in tobacco smoke.

TABLE 5.1 Carcinogenic Chemicals Extracted from Cigarette Smoke[a]

Arsenious oxide	6:7-cyclopenteno-1:2-benzanthracene
1:2-benzanthracene	1:2-5:6-benzanthracene
3:4-benzfluoranthene	3:4-8:9-dibenzpyrene
10:11-benzfluoranthene	3:4-9:10-dibenzpyrene
11:12-benzfluoranthene	3-methylpyrene
1:12-benzperylene	2-naphthol
1:2-benzpyrene	chrysene
3:4-benzpyrene	

---

[a] All of these chemicals have been shown, either by observation of people exposed to them or by animal experiments, to cause cancer.

In addition to these known carcinogens, cigarette smoke contains many substances which have not yet been tested to determine whether they are or are not carcinogens. Also present are hydrocarbons, chemicals which are closely related to the hydrocarbons in gasoline. As explained in the "Solvents" section of Chapter 2, the long-term drug effects of hydrocarbon inhalation may also cause death. Some of the chemicals of this hydrocarbon group are known carcinogens and the remainder are suspected carcinogens.

When a person inhales cigarette smoke, the smoke passes down the trachea (windpipe) to the bronchial tubes and into the lungs. The drawing of the lungs in Figure 5.2 shows that each bronchial tube is wider at each fork. The air or smoke slows down as it enters this region of greater width and deposits particles it may contain. This process is much the same as that of a river that deposits its sediment in the form of a delta where the river broadens into a lake or ocean. The exposure of the bronchial tubes to the particles (including carcinogens) contained in cigarette smoke is thus greatest at the points where the tube is widest. Autopsies of hundreds of human lungs have shown that it is precisely in these areas of maximum exposure that precancerous changes are most likely to take place—and where lung cancers are most likely to appear. Figure 5.3 shows the precancerous changes and the progression through the epithelium of the bronchial tubes which results in lung cancer.

Smoking also causes damage to the protective mechanisms in the lungs. The lining of the bronchial tubes is normally moist. It is covered with mucus that is produced by cells along the surface of the tubes. Many of the surface cells also contain small whiplike fringes called "cilia" (see Figures 5.3 and 5.4) which, with a back-and-forth waving motion, propel the mucus upward and outward toward the throat. Any irritating or poisonous particles or dust entering the bronchial tubes or lungs are trapped in the mucus and propelled by the cilia out of the lungs and bronchial tubes into the throat. This protective mechanism (Figure 5.3) removes unwanted and irritating foreign materials from the easily damaged lungs. Cigarette smoke paralyzes the action of the cilia in the bron-

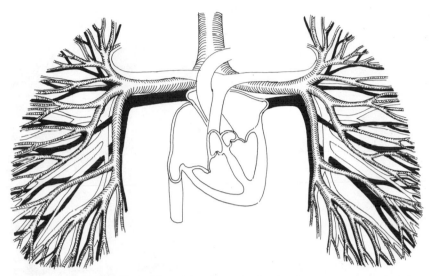

Figure 5.2 *Respiratory system. The bronchial tube begins at the windpipe (trachea), then divides into two tubes (bronchial tubes). Each tube in turn divides as many as 22 times. Because of the treelike structure of the tubes they are sometimes known as the "bronchial tree." The deeper a cigarette smoker inhales, the further along the bronchial tree the smoke proceeds.*

chial tubes. It also causes changes to occur in the lining of the tubes, so that the cilia eventually disappear altogether. Thus some relationships between smoking, lung cancer, and many other respiratory conditions are due, at least in part, to the effects of smoke on the cilia rather than to the direct action of carcinogens. Furthermore, cigarette smoke is itself an irritant. Heavy smokers can feel this irritation in their throats and very often develop "smoker's cough" after a few years of smoking.

Too few smokers realize the degree and extent of health damage associated with cigarette smoking. Early morning hacking and smoker's coughs are so common that millions of Americans consider these normal, rather than signals that warn of damage to the body. Each day in the United States, 250 people die from heart attacks, 100 from lung cancer, and 150 from other cigarette-related diseases. All of the effects of cigarette smoke on the tissues of the body are damaging. The actual role of cigarettes in the production of diseases is great because there is a combination of harmful factors. Any one of them could be responsible for damage, but together they are deadly.

Smoking and Disease

The relationship between smoking and disease has received a great deal of attention. Research first brought to light by the 1964 Surgeon General's

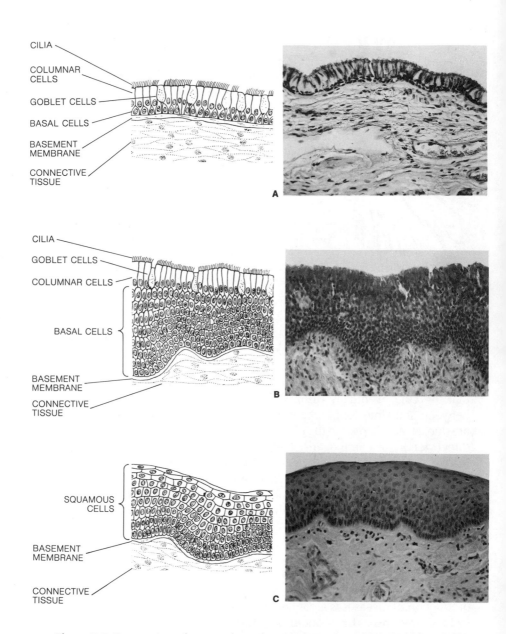

Figure 5.3 *Progression of cancer through epithelium. Bronchial epithelium is the original site of almost all lung cancer, which often develops as shown on the photomicrographs. (A) Normal bronchial epithelium. (B) One of the first effects of smoking becomes evident, an increase in the number of basal cells which is termed* hyperplasia. *(C) The epithelium is lost and the cells become* squamous, *or flattened, and show atypical (darkened) nuclei. (D) This stage is termed carci-*

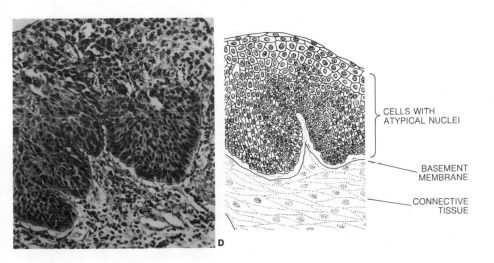

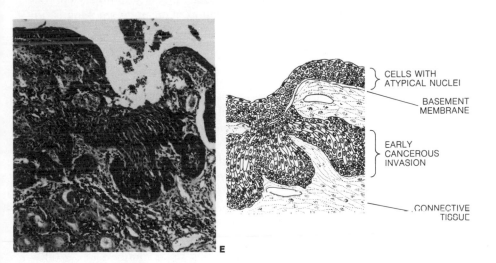

noma in situ. *(E) Finally, a fully developed cancer; when these cells break through the basement membrane the cancer may spread through lungs and to the rest of the body. (From The Effects of Smoking, by Cuyler Hammond. Copyright 1962 by Scientific American Inc. All rights reserved. Photomicrographs by Dr. Oscar Auerbach of the Veterans Administration Hospital, East Orange, N.J.)*

report *Smoking and Health* has shown definite links between smoking and the occurrence of a variety of diseases, some of which are listed in the following sections. This report and subsequent revisions continue to confirm previous findings and suggest additional mechanisms which may cause diseases in smokers. Such a tremendous body of facts had accumulated as early as 1967 that in September of that year the World Conference on Smoking and Health was held in New York City. In the opening address Dr. Luther L. Terry, former Surgeon General of the U.S. Public Health Service, set the theme of the conference and summed up the case against cigarettes when he said:

> We have come to the end of one era in the smoking and health field. The period of uncertainty is over. While science will continue to probe the reason why, there is no longer any doubt that cigarette smoking is a direct threat to the user's health. . . . There was a time when we spoke of the smoking-and-health "controversy." To my mind, the days of argument are over.

Dr. Terry was the U.S. Surgeon General who issued the historic 1964 report.

Evidence about the relationship between smoking and disease is being accumulated at such a rapid pace today that any summary can be only a temporary progress report. Elimination of cigarette smoking is, in fact, the single most important health measure available today for the prevention of disease and premature death in the United States.

Cancer

The amounts of carcinogenic chemicals in tobacco are small, in some cases extremely small. But constant irritation over long periods of time allows these carcinogens to change normal cells into cancerous cells. Such cell changes leading to lung cancer are shown in Figure 5.4. The chances of cancer for nonsmokers and smokers, verified by scientific investigations, are summarized in Table 5.2. This table also shows the increased cancer death rates expected of heavy smokers in any one year.

Dr. Oscar Auerbach has shown conclusively (Figure 5.4) that cancer of the lung (epidermoid carcinoma) is caused by tobacco—largely by cigarette smoking. In the United States in 1914 only 371 deaths were attributed to lung cancer. This number has since climbed to 72,000 deaths in 1974.

Cancers of the tongue, lips, and larynx are also caused by smoking cigar or pipe tobacco as well as cigarette tobacco. Cigarette smoking causes lung cancer because the cigarette smoker inhales. The cigar or pipe smoker usually puffs rather than inhales, unless he has been a heavy cigarette smoker who has switched to a cigar or pipe—in which case, he may continue to inhale. The number of cases of cancer of the esophagus

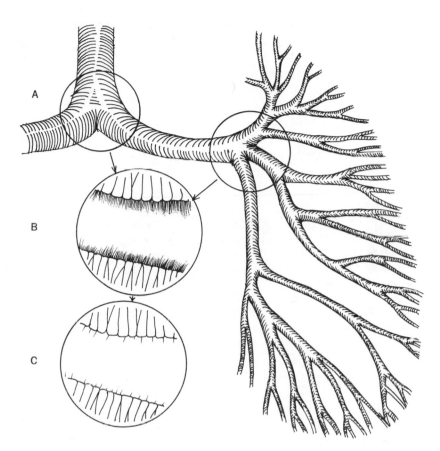

Figure 5.4 *Effects of smoking on the protection mechanisms of the bronchial tubes and lungs. (A) The bronchial tubes are wider just before each fork. Inhaled cigarette smoke entering these regions is slowed down by the greater width; exposure to particles in the smoke is greatest where the tubes are widest. This is where changes leading to cancer are most likely to occur. (B) The surface of the bronchial tubes contain tiny, whiplike fringes called cilia which wave back and forth in such a way as to propel irritating substances out of the lungs. (C) Cigarette smoke paralyzes the action of cilia in the bronchial tubes. As changes occur in the lining of the tubes in response to the smoke, the cilia disappear altogether. The bronchial tubes are then deprived of this protective mechanism.*

and urinary bladder are increasing, and usually patients with these conditions are smokers.

Cardiovascular Diseases

"Cardiovascular disease" is a general name for any condition that impairs the functioning of the circulatory system—the heart and blood vessels. Table 5.3 lists some of the major diseases considered to be specific to the

TABLE 5.2 Expected and Actual Deaths for Smokers of Cigarettes[a]

Underlying Cause of Death	Expected Number of Deaths in the General Population	Actual Number of Smokers Dying in General Population	Increased Ratio of Smoker Deaths
Cancer of lung	170.3	1,833	10.8 to 1
Bronchitis and emphysema	89.5	546	6.1 to 1
Cancer of larynx	14.0	75	5.4 to 1
Oral cancer	37.0	152	4.1 to 1
Cancer of esophagus	33.7	113	3.4 to 1
Stomach and duodenal ulcers	105.1	294	2.8 to 1
Other circulatory diseases	254.0	649	2.6 to 1
Cirrhosis of liver	169.2	379	2.2 to 1
Cancer of bladder	111.6	216	1.9 to 1
Coronary artery disease	6,430.7	11,177	1.7 to 1
Other heart diseases	526.0	868	1.7 to 1
Hypertensive heart disease	409.2	631	1.5 to 1
General arteriosclerosis	210.7	310	1.5 to 1
Cancer of kidney	79.0	120	1.5 to 1
All causes of death[b]	15,653.9	26,223	1.7 to 1

[a]This table shows the expected and actual deaths for smokers of cigarettes only and the ratios of such deaths to expected deaths in the general public. (Adapted from *The Health Consequences of Smoking,* Washington, D.C., U.S. Department of Health, Education, and Welfare, 1969.)

[b]Includes all other causes of death as well as those listed above.

cardiovascular system. The effects of smoking on the heart and blood vessels, in man and experimental animals, result from nicotine.

Recently, studies of large groups of people have shown that cigarette smokers are more likely to die of certain cardiovascular disorders than nonsmokers. Such diseases of the heart and blood vessels are the most common causes of death in our population. A cause-and-effect association has been established between cigarette smoking and the incidence of coronary attacks in humans (see Table 5.2), especially men between 35 and 55 years of age. The risk of death in male cigarette smokers in relation to nonsmokers is greater in middle age than in old age. Statistics prove that smokers are often struck down when they should be most active and enjoying life. They also prove that men who stop smoking have a lower death rate from coronary diseases than those who continue to smoke.

Respiratory Diseases

Smoking is increasingly linked to the development and progression of respiratory (lung-connected) diseases such as *bronchitis* and *emphysema.* These diseases severely disable large numbers of men of working age.

TABLE 5.3 Some Major Diseases Considered to Be Specific to the Cardiovascular System

Disease Category	Definition
Cardiovascular disease	A general name for any condition which impairs the functioning of the circulatory system—the heart and blood vessels
Stroke	An impeded blood supply to some part of the brain caused by a clot, hemorrhage, embolus, or tumor
Coronary heart disease	Any destructive process or disease involving the blood vessels of the heart
Hypertension	Commonly called "high blood pressure." A persistent elevation of blood pressure above the normal range
Arteriosclerosis	Commonly called "hardening of the arteries." Includes any conditions causing artery walls to become thick and hard and lose elasticity
Atherosclerosis	A disease of the arteries in which the inner layer of the wall becomes thick and irregular by deposits of fat. These deposits decrease the inside diameter of the vessel
Congestive heart failure	Failure of the heart which results when the heart can no longer pump and circulate blood efficiently as a result of damage from some form of heart disease

Air pollution and respiratory infections as well as smoking cause and aggravate chronic bronchitis and emphysema. Any pollutant, condition, or infectious agent that can cause permanent damage to the respiratory system can be linked with these diseases. However, smoking causes an increased irritation above and beyond the pollutants and irritants commonly encountered.

BRONCHITIS

When the lining of the bronchial tubes is inflamed to such an extent that air flow is restricted and breathing is labored, bronchitis has developed. Many people suffer brief attacks of acute bronchitis—accompanied by fever, coughing, and spitting—whenever they have severe colds. *Chronic bronchitis* is present when this coughing and spitting continues for months and returns each fall, lasting slightly longer after each cold. This condition is often associated with heavy cigarette smoking. Since people who suffer from chronic bronchitis are commonly smokers, their cough is usually dismissed as a smoker's cough.

EMPHYSEMA

When a person's lungs become enlarged and misshapen to the extent that the transfer of gases to and from the blood is reduced, he has emphysema. Emphysema is a late effect of chronic infection or irritation of the bronchial tubes and lungs. It is a disease that develops over a long period of time. Smoking greatly speeds up the processes leading to emphysema. Many of the people who have emphysema smoke and have been heavy smokers most of their lives.

Maternal Smoking, Pregnancy, and Infant Birth Weight

Since 1970 the percent of women in the United States who smoke has increased from 8 percent of the smoking population to 12 percent. Also, during this period the number of individuals in the 14- to 18-year-old range smoking has increased proportionately. If this trend continues through the 1970s, the heaviest smoking population will be the 25- to 34-year-olds, especially among women. This is during women's major reproductive years. The expectant mother who smokes has more to worry about than the nonsmoking woman. A British study of more than 1,000 mothers showed that one in 5 spontaneous abortions would not have occurred had the mother not smoked regularly during her pregnancy. Smoking women also tend to have babies of lower birth weight, and children of such women are known to have a high incidence of neurological damage and a greater chance of dying during the first year of life. Women who smoke during pregnancy affect two lives, their own and the child's.

Rights of the Nonsmoker

Studies have shown that exposure to a "smoking environment," such as a smoke-filled closed room, automobile, airplane, theater, or restaurant, causes measurable effects in the body, including increased heart rate, higher blood pressure, and an increased amount of carbon dioxide in the blood. Nonsmokers in a closed smoking environment often experience eye and nose irritation, headache, sore throat, coughing, hoarseness, nausea, and dizziness. Because of these unpleasant effects of smoke upon nonsmokers, commercial airlines and interstate buses have separate seating areas for smokers and nonsmokers. Many restaurants and theaters are also setting aside nonsmoking sections. The American Medical Association has asked member doctors to keep people from smoking in their waiting rooms.

Nonsmokers should consider smoking in their presence an act of aggression. Cigarette smokers smoking in a crowded, ill-ventilated room or automobile can raise the level of carbon monoxide to a point dangerous to anyone's health. Experiments show that in a small room, a smoker can raise the level of carbon monoxide to 50 parts per million. At this level, after 1½ hours, a nonsmoker can have trouble discriminating time intervals and visual and auditory cues. This can affect vision and the ability to drive safely. Nonsmokers have as much of a right to clean air as smokers have to fill the air with smoke. *Make smoking in your presence socially unacceptable;* you will be doing everyone a favor.

The Smoking Habit

As early as 1967, the World Conference on Smoking and Health concluded that the individuals who exhibit a continuing need to smoke show a dependence similar to all other major forms of drug dependence.

Of all the substances known to be present in tobacco smoke, nicotine alone can produce the drug dependence associated with habitual smoking. When a smoker's nicotine level declines 20 or 30 minutes after using a cigarette, he begins to feel subtle withdrawal symptoms that cause him to smoke another cigarette.

Only plants containing chemicals, such as nicotine, which produce drug dependence have been abused habitually over long periods of time. Besides tobacco, these plants include coffee, tea, and cocoa (caffeine); betel nut (acrecoline); marijuana or cannabis (cannabinols); khat (pseudo-ephedrine); opium (narcotic alkaloids); and coca leaves (cocaine).

A person's first experiences with smoking tobacco are usually tied to psychological and social pressures. A person with this extent of dependence falls into a category in which he can smoke or not at will. As a result, he may have periods of smoking and abstention throughout his lifetime. The smoking periods will be in response to peer, social, or psychological pressures. But the continued use of tobacco if encouraged and kept up, is then made habitual by the dependence-producing effects of nicotine on the body. These effects occur in a number of tissues and organs, including the central nervous system. The effect of tobacco on the smoker seems to be that of a stimulant and can be followed by depression, depending upon the person's real or imagined reaction to smoking. But whatever the particular reaction, nicotine-free tobacco, or cigarettes made from other plant materials (such as lettuce), do not satisfy smokers.

The evidence seems to indicate that there are two basic groups of dependent smokers. In one group the dependence is psychosocial and giving up smoking is relatively easy, involving little physical discomfort. The other group of smokers seems to be physically dependent on tobacco. In this case the dependence is harder to break, and withdrawal symptoms, while not adequately described, are present. Tobacco is not legally classified as a dangerous drug, for the most part because it does not cause the drastic mood modifications or behavior changes found among those who abuse the more potent drugs. But although the immediate effects of tobacco are mild, the overall, long-range effects are drastic. Because of continuing physical damage to the body and health of the individual, its use is drug abuse.

How Smoking Begins

As mentioned earlier, the years from the early teens to the early twenties are when a majority of people begin to develop the habits and social patterns that will cause them to start to smoke or become smokers later.

Two factors help to explain why young people begin smoking: (1) the desire to imitate, and (2) the wish for adult status. In many cases there is a relationship among smoking, a need for status among friends and peers, increased self-assurance, and a desire to feel or appear more mature. Psychiatrists see smoking behavior as an accelerated striving for social status in the sense that the beginning smoker is often trying to show an adultlike need for personal and social standing.

As shown in Figure 5.5, a strong relationship has been found to exist between parents' and youngsters' smoking habits. It seems that the smoking of parents affects the age at which children take up smoking more than it influences whether the children will become smokers or nonsmokers. Consequently, many authorities believe that the most effective way to cut down smoking among young people is to cut out smoking among their parents.

It should be noted that many studies reveal that the health damage is greater among individuals who start cigarette smoking early in life than among those who start later. Also, the ability of an individual to stop smoking whenever he desires is clearly related to how long he has been smoking.

There have been a few scientific studies of the personal and social reasons for smoking. The following are some of the major personal and social characteristics that tend to be found among smokers as a group.

Social Status

Evidence suggests that early smoking is linked with self-esteem and status-seeking in ambitious young people. The pattern or style of living an individual seeks within his family, community, and peer group seems to have a strong influence on his smoking behavior. A permissive cultural climate (one in which smoking is readily permitted) results in an increase of smoking among young people, especially those who tend to conform to the society's liberal standards.

Personality and Smoking

Although no "smoker personality" has been shown to exist, certain common personality traits have been reported among smokers. Smokers tend to be extroverted (outgoing) people who place perhaps too strong an

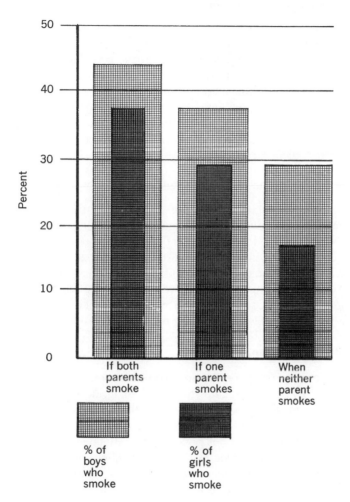

Figure 5.5 *Smoking habits of teenagers and parents. A large majority of teenage smokers come from homes where one or both parents smoke. (Courtesy American Cancer Society, Profile 1967.)*

emphasis on immediate pleasure. Because smokers often take a large part in various social activities, they are placed in situations that reinforce their smoking habits. They are also more open to suggestions from social influences and friends.

Generally, it seems that different personality types tend to establish specific smoking habits. The pipe and cigar smoker often looks for sedation in smoking; the cigarette smoker more often wants stimulation. Consequently, very few cigarette smokers can change to pipes or cigars and be as satisfied as they were with cigarettes.

Psychoanalytic Theory of Smoking

Some psychoanalysts have set forth the theory that smoking, like thumb sucking, is a return to an infantile (regressive) oral activity related to the infant's pleasure in sucking at his mother's breast. It is claimed that male thumb suckers are very likely to smoke, drink, or be overweight in later years. When these individuals stop smoking, they frequently show increased food consumption, weight gain, or dependence on chewing gum to suppress this oral need. However, other experts argue that this analysis is not in itself sufficient and that smoking patterns can be better explained by other psychological factors.

Smoking as a Response to Stress and Tension

Stress seems to be conducive to smoking, as it is to so many other habits. Tense or challenging situations contribute to the beginning of the smoking habit, its continuation, and to the number of cigarettes a person consumes. Increased experiences of stress among young people, together with social situations favorable to smoking, may set off first experiments with smoking. Later, tense or strained situations tend to reinforce or strengthen the habit. By the time a smoker has developed a well-established habit, he may respond to even the slightest tension by reaching for a cigarette.

Smoking and Achievement

Intelligence does not seem to be a factor in whether or not individuals take up smoking. But evidence indicates that smokers tend to achieve less in schoolwork than nonsmokers. The reason for this tendency is extremely hard to analyze. It is unlikely that smoking, by itself, is responsible for unsatisfactory schoolwork. But it is possible that whatever causes an individual to smoke may also reduce his interest in school, for example, the increased social activity that smokers seek at this age. Smoking might also result from frustration or might be a reaction to failure.

Breaking the Habit

There is good evidence that the decision to stop smoking is related to the forces which led to the habit, the number of cigarettes smoked per day, and the duration of the smoking habit.

The ability of an individual to stop smoking has consistently been found to be highest among those who started late in life, those who have smoked for the least number of years, and those whose daily cigarette consumption has been low.

The most frequent reasons for smokers to stop, or not to continue to smoke after the first trials, are lack of satisfaction or actual dislike for smoking. These reasons are interesting because they are not the reasons young people give for not taking up smoking. Their reasons are connected with health, aesthetics, and morals.

Among adult smokers who quit, the most frequent reason given is "various health reasons." Relatively few refer to specific diseases such as lung cancer, emphysema, or cardiovascular diseases. Other reasons for quitting include the expense of cigarettes, moral considerations, and a "test of will power."

For a person to stop smoking he must first stop ignoring the health dangers of smoking and accept his smoking as a personal problem which he must conquer. Then, everything possible should be done to quit smoking, even if for a limited time.

This has been done in a number of ways, but the most successful methods fall into the following categories: (1) withdrawal clinics or smokers' clinics, often conducted by hospitals or health organizations; (2) individual medical care provided by physicians or psychologists and programs of self-help based upon books, magazines, lectures, pamphlets, etc. Such literature is available from the American Cancer Society, the Heart Association, and many others; (3) commercial clinics and programs that use hypnosis or aversion therapy.

Withdrawal clinics are actually group therapy sessions where physicians and health professionals conduct a series of sessions that explain the health hazards of smoking. Often a psychologist conducts part of the session to help reinforce the individuals and suggest methods of stopping or reducing their smoking. The participants are encouraged to explain how well they are doing and to make suggestions to other members of the group.

Once the group has been established there are three goals to accomplish to reach success: (1) to assist the individual in building strong motivation to stop smoking; (2) to confront the individual's attitudes toward smoking constructively, especially those relating to events and feelings associated with the withdrawal experiences taking place within the group; and (3) to provide support and guidance during and immediately following the period of withdrawal from tobacco.

Preparations containing lobeline, a drug with actions resembling nicotine, are now sold over the counter. The smoker takes such lobeline compounds in decreasing doses once he has cut down on his consumption of tobacco. While these drugs may, as claimed, help the smoker to break his dependence on nicotine, they do not replace the *dependence* of smoking. Thus the smoker may find, when he tries to stop, that he acquires new habits to replace smoking. To keep his hands busy, he may become a "fiddler." To satisfy his oral need, he may overeat or become a nail biter. But because these habits are seldom as satisfying to him as smoking, he more often than not returns to tobacco.

In programs using hypnosis, an individual is given the hypnotic suggestion that cigarettes taste unpleasant. This suggestion may be repeated once or twice a month with continuing visits to the clinic. In clinics using aversion therapy the individual is subjected to an electric shock each time he takes a puff on a cigarette. In time he will feel the shock whenever he puffs on a cigarette. If this is unpleasant enough to him he will stop smoking.

In conclusion, though breaking the smoking habit is seldom easy, the effort required may be handsomely rewarded in added years of good health. If you smoke—quit now. If you don't smoke—don't start.

Summary

I. Cigarette smoking is by far the commonest form of drug abuse in the United States today

II. Composition and effects of tobacco smoke

A. Tobacco contains more than a hundred known chemical compounds
B. The effects of these chemicals include:

1. Table 5.1 lists some of the carcinogens (cancer-producing) chemicals in tobacco smoke
2. Long-term inhalation of "solvents" (see Chapter 2) may also cause death
3. Figure 5.3 shows the progression within the bronchial epithelium which results in lung cancer from smoking

III. Smoking and disease

A. Cancer—Table 5.2 shows the increased death rate from cancer expected of heavy smokers in any one year
B. Cardiovascular diseases—cigarette smokers are more likely to die of certain cardiovascular disorders than nonsmokers
C. Respiratory diseases—cigarette smoking is increasingly linked to the development of respiratory diseases such as bronchitis and emphysema

1. Bronchitis is inflammation of the bronchial tubes
2. Emphysema results when a person's lungs become enlarged and misshapen to such an extent that the transfer of gases to and from the blood is reduced

D. Maternal smoking, pregnancy, and infant birth weight

1. Smoking women show an increased spontaneous abortion rate
2. Smoking women have a high incidence of lower birth weight babies

IV. Rights of the nonsmoker

A. Everyone exposed to a "smoking environment" such as closed rooms, automobiles, buses, airplanes, theaters, or restaurants shows a measurable effect in his or her body
B. Nonsmokers should consider smoking in their presence "an act of aggression"

V. The smoking habit—drug dependence

    A. Individuals who have a continuing need to smoke show a dependence similar to all other major forms of drug dependence

        1. Nicotine seems to be the chemical producing the drug dependence associated with smoking

        2. Only plants containing chemicals which produce drug dependence have been abused habitually throughout history

    B. Evidence indicates that there are two basic groups of dependent smokers

        1. In one group the dependence is more psychological, and giving up smoking is relatively easy

        2. The other group seems to have a physical dependence on tobacco, which is harder to break

    C. Tobacco is not legally classified as a dangerous drug because it does not cause the drastic mood-modifications or behavior changes found among abusers of illegal drugs

VI. Smoking begins—the years from the early teens to the early twenties are the years in which a majority of people begin to smoke

    A. Social Status—evidence suggests that early smoking is linked to status-seeking by young people

    B. Personality and smoking

        1. No smoker personality has been shown to exist

        2. Smokers do tend to be extroverted people who place too strong an emphasis on immediate pleasure

    C. Psychoanalytic theory of smoking sets forth that smoking, like thumb sucking, is a return to infantile oral activity related to the infant's pleasure in sucking at the mother's breast

    D. Smoking as a response to stress and tension. Tense or challenging situations contribute to the beginning of smoking, its continuation, and the number of cigarettes smoked

    E. Smoking and achievement—smokers tend to achieve less in schoolwork than nonsmokers

VII. Breaking the habit

    A. The decision to stop smoking is related to the forces which led to the habit, number of cigarettes smoked, and the duration of the habit

    B. Ability to stop smoking is highest among those who started late in life, have smoked the fewest years, and smoke few cigarettes daily

    C. For a person to stop smoking he must first stop ignoring the health dangers of smoking and accept his smoking as a personal problem which he must conquer

    D. There are a number of ways to quit smoking

· **1.** Withdrawal or "smoker's" clinics

2. Individual or self-help programs based upon books, magazines, or lectures

3. Commercial clinics and programs using hypnosis or aversion therapy

E. Though breaking the habit is seldom easy the effort is rewarded in added years of good health

Questions for Review

1. How many individuals smoke in the United States?

2. What is the dependence-producing potential of smoking?

3. What is the chance an individual can stop smoking whenever he would like?

4. Outline the precancerous changes in the progression of lung cancer associated with smoking.

5. What is the degree and extent of health damage associated with cigarette smoking?

6. Which diseases are most closely related to smoking? How severe can these diseases be?

7. What should be the "rights" of a nonsmoker when in the presence of a smoker?

Chapter 6
LAWS AND TREATMENT

Narcotics began arriving in our country even before the founding of the republic. By the 1800s, narcotics were taken as constituents of patent medicines and cure-alls. This use increased greatly with the invention of the hypodermic needle and syringe just before the Civil War. Doctors actually encouraged their patients to buy this device and to use narcotics on a "do-it-yourself" basis. The miracle medicines, elixirs, and tonics, which contained large amounts of narcotics—usually opium preparations—were easy to obtain and were reputed to be cures for everything.

By the end of the Civil War, thousands of soldiers had received injections of narcotics to relieve their suffering from wounds and sickness. Many became addicted to these drugs. Then, with the growth of advertising and the promotion of patent medicines containing narcotics, great numbers of people took such medicines and became addicted to them. Some, having discovered the fact that these medicines contained opium, bought and used straight opium. Narcotic abuse climbed steeply even after 1914, when the first effective drug control laws were enacted. There was very little actual reduction in the abuse of narcotics until the Federal Bureau of Narcotics was established in 1930 to enforce the earlier narcotics laws and apprehend violators. The name of this agency has since been changed to the Bureau of Narcotics and Dangerous Drugs (BNDD).

The major narcotic abused today is heroin, which was first introduced in 1898 as a cure for morphine addiction. In recent years other potent drugs have been produced that are now used and abused to an even greater extent than the narcotics. There are more mood-modifying drugs being developed today than any other group of drugs. Also, millions of people legitimately use amphetamines (in diet and "pep" pills) and barbiturates (mainly sleeping pills). The possibility of abuse is increasing greatly by the familiarity of legally used drugs and the availability of new and more potent drugs.

Legal Control of Drugs

One philosophy of drug abuse behavior sees a drug abuser as a criminal whose criminality manifests itself in drug offenses. His involvement in the use, possession, sale, or theft of drugs is regarded as a part of predictable criminal behavior.

Federal Drug Controls

The early federal laws made no attempt to define legally or medically the drugs that were controlled. Instead they specified that *opium* and its derivatives (the *opiates*), *coca leaves* and their derivatives (including *cocaine*), *marijuana,* and *peyote (mescaline)* were "habit-forming narcotic drugs." Also, specific synthetic drugs that "produce sleep or stupor and relieve pain" were declared to be narcotics.

In 1970 a new trend in drug control was established when Congress passed the *Comprehensive Drug Abuse Prevention and Control Act.* This law completely redesigned the older drug laws in an effort to adapt federal drug law to the drug abuse problems of the 1970s. It divides all drugs into five classes whose illegal manufacture, distribution, possession, and possession for sale are controlled by the federal government. An outline of the five classes of drugs and the penalties for violations are shown in Table 6.1.

Class I drugs are considered to have the highest potential for being abused because of their mood-modifying qualities. They carry the most severe penalties, are regarded as the most dangerous, and are outlawed from being used medically in the United States. Class II drugs have the same high potential for abuse as Class I drugs, but are used in medicine. Class III drugs are considered to have a potential for abuse, but not as high as Class I and II drugs; penalties have been reduced. Class IV drugs have a lower potential for abuse; their penalties are further reduced. Class V drugs have the lowest potential for abuse, and the penalties are the mildest.

The maximum penalty for simple possession of any drug is one year for a first offense and 2 years for a second conviction. Also, an individual under 21 years of age, convicted of simple possession (first offense), may be placed on probation without formal sentencing, and if he successfully completes the probation, the official arrest, trial records, and conviction can be erased from his record.

This law gives the U.S. Attorney General (with consent of a panel of experts) the power to decide which class a drug belongs in on the basis of its potential for abuse. Enforcement of such federal drug laws is the responsibility of the BNDD of the U.S. Justice Department.

A controversial aspect of this federal law was the "no-knock" provision, which allowed police to enter and search a home or room without the ordinary warrant or without knocking—if there was reason to believe that drugs were on the premises. In 1973 this provision of the Comprehensive Drug Abuse Act was repealed by Congress, because of some very controversial searches of innocent people's homes. Consequently, today a warrant must be issued before agents search a home or room for drugs.

State Drug Controls

In 1932 a model *Uniform State Narcotics Law* was submitted to several states. Since that time this law or similar laws have been enacted by the state legislatures of most states. States are constantly reexamining their laws and making extensive changes. Prosecution to the limit of the law is rare. Also, judges have greater flexibility in interpreting and applying state laws. Although in the past the practice of most states has been to remodel old laws, most states are now designing their laws to fit their own unique circumstances or are establishing laws similar to the *Federal Drug Abuse Prevention and Control Act of 1970* (Table 6.1).

If you would like to know about the drug laws of your state, your local district attorney's office will answer any of your questions.

Juveniles and the Law

Being placed under arrest and processed through juvenile court can create many problems in a person's future because of the various records that accompany such arrests and proceedings. The job he desires may become unavailable to him if he has been arrested, even if his case was handled in juvenile court. Certain professions (such as law and medicine) will be ruled out. Joining a particular branch of the military may also be difficult or impossible.

The specific conditions and proceedings concerning juveniles vary from state to state, but individuals from 18 to 21 years of age are usually subject to the same state laws regarding marijuana, narcotics, dangerous drugs, and other violations as are adults.

Often when a juvenile (a person under 18 years of age) is arrested and taken to the police station, one of three things may happen, depending on the juvenile's background and previous record, his attitude, and the nature of the particular offense: (1) His parents are called to the station, the situation explained to them, and he is released to them without any further action. (2) He is released to his parents, and the police then submit a petition to the juvenile court explaining the offense. Such a petition is

TABLE 6.1 Drug Schedules and Penalties for Violation of

Drug Schedule	Potential for Abuse	Medical Use	Production Controls	Examples of Drugs in Each Class
Class I	High	No medical use	Yes	Opium derivatives and hallucinogenic drugs: heroin, marijuana, THC, LSD, mescaline
Class II	High	Medical use	Yes	Medically used narcotics and injectable metamphetamines: morphine, cocaine, methadone
Class III	High but less than Classes I and II	Medical use	No controls	"Mild" narcotics: codeine, amphetamines, and barbiturates
Class IV	Low	Medical use	No controls	"Mild" barbiturates, chloral hydrate, meprobamate
Class V	Low, less than Class IV	Medical use	No controls	"Low" percentage narcotic mixtures, tranquilizers

*The schedules and penalties may be changed by the U.S. Attorney General at any time.

a juvenile equivalent of a criminal complaint issued against an adult. (3) He is detained by the police while they are applying for a petition to be submitted to the juvenile court.

After hearing the evidence, the court will either dismiss the petition or find it to be true. If it is found to be true, the minor will reappear in court for disposition of his case, which is equivalent to an adult appearing at a probation and sentencing hearing after having been convicted of a crime. Generally, there is far greater flexibility in the handling of minors than there is in handling adults. The three most common results of a juvenile conviction are: (1) he is sent home but will be under the supervision of a probation officer; (2) he is sent to a camp maintained by the probation department; or (3) if the minor has previously been on probation or in a

Comprehensive Drug Abuse Prevention and Control Act*

Drug Schedule	Maximum Penalties for Manufacturing, Distribution, and Sales	Maximum Penalties for Simple Illegal Possession
Class I	Narcotics First offense: 3 to 15 years, $15,000 fine Second and subsequent offenses: 6 to 30 years, $50,000 fine	
Class II	Nonnarcotics First offense: 2 to 5 years, $15,000 fine Second and subsequent offenses: 4 to 10 years, $30,000 fine	First offense: 1 year, $5,000 fine Probation may be given Second offense: 2 years, $10,000 fine
Class III	First offense: 2 to 5 years, $15,000 fine Second and subsequent offenses: 4 to 10 years, $20,000 fine	
Class IV	First offense: 1 to 3 years, $10,000 fine Second and subsequent offenses: 2 to 6 years, $20,000 fine	
Class V	First offense: up to 1 year, $5,000 fine Second and subsequent offenses: Up to 2 years, $10,000 fine	

camp and is over 16 years of age, the juvenile court may conclude that he is "incorrigible," and he is prosecuted as an adult.

In some states youths between 18 and 21 who commit crimes are initially processed as adults. However, after a complaint has been issued either by the district attorney or the city attorney, the judge in the adult court can refer the matter to juvenile court if he feels that it is warranted. It is then up to the juvenile court judge either to accept the case in juvenile court or to refuse to accept it. In the latter event, the 18- to 21-year-old defendant will be sent back to the adult court and tried as an adult.

Legal Control of Drug Abusers

Most drug control laws do not attack the actual drug problem but just jail the offender. The misuse of drugs is a medical problem with legal consequences and should be attacked as such a problem. We should study compulsive users, addicts, and alcoholics for common traits to find the conditions, medical, social, and psychological, that produce drug abuse behavior. Then, possibly, we can arrive at workable methods of prevention or treatment, rehabilitation, and control.

Enforcement of drug laws is the only means of control available until research tells us how to prevent drug abuse behavior. Different kinds of drug abusers need different kinds of treatment and differing amounts of control. A drug user should voluntarily enter a treatment program that offers the amount of control he needs before the necessary laws are invoked upon him. Private treatment programs usually control individuals through the family or peer populations. Individuals lacking the self-control to stay in a private treatment program will always be the ones who are placed within the legal control of public treatment programs.

Federal Narcotic Addict Rehabilitation Act of 1966

The Federal Narcotic Addict Rehabilitation Act of 1966 helps states and communities to treat drug abusers. An eligible person charged with a crime may be told by a judge that the criminal charge will be held in abeyance if he will submit to a medical examination to determine whether he is an addict and could be rehabilitated through treatment. He has 5 days to make a decision. If he elects to apply for treatment he then is retained in a hospital for not more than 60 days for examination purposes. If he is found to need treatment and is considered suitable, he will be placed in a state hospital or state drug treatment facility through a *commitment procedure.*

CRIMINAL COMMITMENT FOR DRUG ABUSE

If a judge believes an eligible *convicted* criminal offender is an addict or is in danger of becoming an addict, he may order him to be examined and committed to a treatment program (in a state facility) for an indeterminate period of time. The commitment cannot be more than 10 years, but must be more than 6 months. After treatment the individual may be released under the supervision of a probation or parole officer.

CIVIL COMMITMENT FOR DRUG ABUSE

Civil commitment is a legal mechanism used instead of a criminal commitment to ensure control over drug abusers during rehabilitation—first in a treatment institution, later in a halfway house, and still later in the community under the supervision of a probation or parole officer. The significant aspect of a civil commitment is that the drug abuser does not establish a criminal record.

An individual related to an addict may volunteer him for a civil commitment by filing a petition, through the police, with the federal district attorney, who may then order the drug abuser to submit to a physical examination and be committed to a drug treatment program.

Drug Abuse Therapy

Most drug users (experimenters and occasional users) given adequate supervision will eventually give up the use of illegal drugs after a period of drug-free living, if only to avoid an involuntary return to an institution.

Medical authorities feel that the compulsive drug user, addict, or alcoholic is emotionally disturbed and often physically ill from the toxic effects of the drug he is abusing. He needs treatment for the physical effects of the drug and psychological help, often continuing throughout life, to keep him from going back to drug abuse when he leaves the hospital. Drug therapy must be aimed at the psychological and sociological problems of the individual abusing drugs and his family. Many drug abusers, like alcoholics, would prefer not to stop using drugs or drinking, but to return to controlled, moderate drug use or drinking. But most authorities are convinced that at the present time, the return to controlled drug use is an unrealistic or most often an impossible goal. Very few compulsive drug users or alcoholics have been able to return to controlled drug use. Such individuals must also be wary of their use of prescription and certain over-the-counter drugs for medicinal purposes.

Emergency Therapy

When an individual under the influence of drugs comes to the attention of a hospital staff or a private physician, it is usually an emergency situation. Under these conditions the physician needs to know certain information to save the patient from death.

First, the physician needs the name of the drug or combination of drugs the individual has used. Because the individual may be unconscious, semicoherent, disoriented, frightened, or behaving as an acute psychotic, this is often difficult to determine. The accounts of friends, the contents of the user's pockets, or the surroundings under which the adverse reaction occurred help the physician to evaluate the situation.

The next phase, if the patient is conscious, is the "talk-down" phase. During this time a quiet, "cool" environment and a well-established rapport between the physician and patient is valuable. Often little more than acceptance and reassurance is necessary to relieve the anxiety and fear that the drug user is experiencing.

Use of Drugs

Accepted medical procedure for treating drug abusers often involves mood-modifying drugs. This may begin with the withdrawal phase and continue throughout the treatment program.

WITHDRAWAL THERAPY

When certain groups of drugs, such as opiates, barbiturates, or alcohol, are used several times a day, the body cells of the user become *tolerant* (see page 8) to and physically dependent upon the drug. When such drugs are withdrawn from the individual, the tolerant cells and body systems must return to normal. The symptoms produced while these cells and body systems are returning to normal are called *withdrawal symptoms* or the *abstinence syndrome*. The specific symptoms produced during the withdrawal from alcohol or barbiturates is termed *alcohol-barbiturate abstinence syndrome*, while withdrawal from narcotics or solvents produces *narcotic-solvent abstinence syndrome*.

Abrupt withdrawal, the "cold turkey" treatment, is uncomfortable, painful, and dangerous. Withdrawing an individual from an addicting drug by gradually reducing the dosage and substituting less potent drugs greatly reduces the severity of the abstinence syndrome symptoms.

The narcotic *methadone* may be substituted for a narcotic such as heroin or morphine during withdrawal treatment. In barbiturate withdrawal the drug *pentobarbital* can be used as a substitute drug. During late-phase alcoholism (phase VI), the alcoholic should also be gradually withdrawn from alcohol. *Paraldehyde* may be used as an alcohol substitute. To stop drinking or taking drugs, either voluntarily or involuntarily, involves a risk of serious withdrawal symptoms. The alcoholic, addict, or compulsive drug abuser needs medical attention, often including hospitalization, during his sobering up or "coming down" period.

DRUG THERAPY FOR ALCOHOLISM

Many drugs have been tried in treating alcoholics, with variable success. Tranquilizing drugs are sometimes effective in decreasing anxiety, delirium tremens, and the restlessness common to all drug abusers.

In drug-induced *aversion therapy,* the individual is given drugs which make him sick if he drinks beverages containing alcohol. Daily use of a drug such as *Antabuse* (disulfiram) causes a highly unpleasant body reaction (including nausea and vomiting) if any alcohol is also ingested. This drug may be taken for months or even years, but the alcoholic must really want to stop drinking. Otherwise, he will just stop taking the Antabuse.

Another type of aversion therapy is to give the alcoholic a drink of liquor along with a drug which makes him sick. After several of these treatments, he may develop a conditioned reflex so that an alcoholic drink alone will make him sick.

MAINTENANCE TREATMENT

Because of the short-acting ups and downs of psychoactive drugs such as heroin, a drug user thinks about drugs and obtaining drugs all the time. The first step in treatment should eliminate the need for psychoactive drugs and establish normal social functioning, perhaps by giving the individual a daily "maintenance" dose of a drug which blocks the psychotropic effects of the drug being abused. Methadone and *acetylmethadol* have these blocking properties.

Individuals on a methadone maintenance program are given one oral dose daily. Acetylmethadol is longer lasting, and in such programs a patient needs to take it only 2 or 3 times a week. With maintenance drugs individuals have been successful in staying away from psychotropic drugs and have become acceptable citizens by combining maintenance programs with psychotherapy and rehabilitation education.

NARCOTIC ANTAGONISTS

Another approach is the use of *narcotic antagonists*—drugs chemically and structurally so like narcotics that they can apparently occupy the place in the nervous system where narcotics act, without producing the euphoria and other effects associated with drug abuse. Three of the more important antagonists are *Nalline, cyclazocine,* and *naloxine.*

While someone is taking several daily doses of a narcotic antagonist, he will not feel the effects of a narcotic, nor will he become addicted to it. Thus, antagonists may provide a means of "unlearning" drug-using behavior.

Drugs in treatment programs make it possible for individuals to continue working and participating in a rehabilitation program before they take the drastic step of trying to live without drugs. To be effective, therapeutic drugs must be part of a broad program of psychological and social rehabilitation.

Psychotherapy

The basis of all drug abuse treatment programs is psychotherapy. The approach may be either a superficial emotional reinforcement of the individual or a deep exploration of the subconscious mind to uncover underlying emotional conflicts that may be contributing to the individual's reasons for abusing drugs. For success, the therapist must have an unusually good understanding of the drug abuser. It is often difficult for someone who has never abused drugs to understand what it means to be a drug abuser. Forms of group psychotherapy seem especially successful because drug abusers do tend to understand each other. Such understanding is the basis of programs such as Alcoholics Anonymous, Narcotics Anonymous, Teen Challenge, therapeutic communities, and most public treatment programs.

Therapeutic Communities

A distinct drug treatment approach involves the establishment of complex social systems that are run almost entirely by ex-addicts. The individual lives, works, and maintains almost all of his social contacts within the therapeutic community. Individuals are not required to remain at these centers and are free to leave at any time. However, to stay, they must at all times demonstrate a willingness to participate and conform to community rules.

Many former compulsive drug abusers and alcoholics are able to remain drug-free and function productively in such communities. The group and individual interaction has as its goal exposing and correcting the immature and exploitive attitudes that underlie compulsive drug abuse.

The therapeutic community is often criticized for the inability of its residents to reenter the community at large. Some, such as Synanon, no longer encourage addicts to leave the community and reenter society. Experience indicates that addicts often require the permanent support of a therapeutic community to prevent them from returning to drug abuse. This was first shown with alcoholics who need an association with Alcoholics Anonymous throughout life.

Alcoholics Anonymous

The most successful approach to the problem of drug abuse today is Alcoholics Anonymous (AA). Alcoholics Anonymous is a loosely organized group of nondrinking alcoholics whose sole purpose is to help its members stay sober. In a large city, there may be groups meeting every night of the week. There are even special groups for young (teenage) alcoholics and for spouses and children of alcoholics. Alcoholics Anonymous is listed in the telephone book and will answer any request for information.

The approach taken by AA is a variety of group therapy, in which members find a deep personal, emotional, and spiritual experience through association with other sober alcoholics. Despite popular belief, all but the very newest members at a meeting are sober. At a typical AA meeting, several members may stand and informally tell their stories of trouble and misery during their drinking years and how AA has helped them. The new member, usually defensive and skeptical, hears experiences similar to his own and often finds that he can identify strongly with a person who has just stood and made the statement, "I am an alcoholic." The new member learns to think of alcoholism as an illness and finds encouragement in seeing alcoholics who have remained sober for years. The new member takes an important step when he admits his own alcoholism. He can now feel a part of AA and often finds himself eager to help other alcoholics regain their sobriety.

It should be emphasized that AA does not claim to cure the alcoholic, only to help *control* his illness, much as insulin does not cure diabetes but does enable the diabetic to live a normal life. There have been many cases of AA members becoming overconfident after many years of sobriety and attempting social drinking, with disastrous results. AA firmly believes that no alcoholic can ever return to moderate social drinking.

Also it must be stressed that AA cannot help the alcoholic who does not fulfill three essential qualifications: (1) a sincere desire to stop drinking, (2) a willingness to admit that he, by himself, is unable to solve his drinking problem—that he must have help, and (3) the ability to be honest with himself.

Abuse Prevention Programs

While the P.T.A., Lions, Rotary Club, and Kiwanis International are among the organizations presenting valuable drug-abuse prevention programs, one of the most promising new programs for teenagers is DAWN TODAY, Inc. DAWN (Developing Adolescents Without Narcotics) was founded in a Los Angeles high school but meets off-campus. DAWN's carefully selected adult counselors work with a small number of teenagers at a time. Those involved in DAWN range from young people who are intensely habituated to drugs to those who are not involved at all. One of the founders has said: "We don't see drugs as the problem. They are just a symptom. If it weren't drugs it might be something else as a manifestation of their problem."

Another new and apparently successful program is the Narcotic Hot Line, an answering service with many community resources available through a referral list. Most callers remain anonymous while counselors first talk with them, but many of them later return for consultation and guidance.

All of these programs recognize the fact that many young people are or will be involved with drugs. Aside from attempting to inform these users and potential users of the dangers of drug abuse, they seek to offer the criteria for making alternate decisions about drugs and the way of life that often accompanies their abuse.

The Return to Society

Because the social pressures that led the addict to drug abuse are still likely to be present when he returns to society, he faces many problems upon his return. These social problems, moreover, are often compounded by legal and economic difficulties.

If he has returned to his community in gradual stages, or if he has not established a criminal record, he has a much better chance of making an adjustment. Ideally, he should first make short visits to his home, then he may live in a halfway house, a work camp, a parish house, or a day-night hospital. These facilities provide the addict with social, therapeutic, and vocational services. Too often, however, the individual simply leaves the hospital—or, more often, the jail—and is "dumped back onto the street." Consequently, it is only a very short time before he is again using drugs.

If the individual has been convicted of a felony, he may face further problems. Such a conviction can mean loss of voting rights, loss of the right to hold public office, and loss of the right to obtain certain state licenses such as a license to sell liquor, to practice law, or to dispense narcotics. Very often an individual convicted of a felony may be required to register with the local police department, or with the Office of Immigration whenever he leaves or enters this and other countries.

Such a felony conviction can also hamper the individual economically. He is unable to be bonded and cannot hold positions that require a bond. Because of this and his inability to acquire certain security clearances through the government, he is also excluded from employment in defense establishments or with defense contractors. Many employers make it a policy to refuse to hire any person with a felony conviction on his record.

In any case, the return to society from drug addiction is not easy. The number of addicts who actually return to a drug-free existence is small when compared with the number who fail. Fortunately, programs are being developed to assist addicts in their attempts to return to their communities, and, perhaps more important, to cope with drugs. A number of addict-directed rehabilitation programs, such as Encounter, Narcotics Anonymous, and Teen Challenge, which is mainly composed of teenagers who have been involved with drugs, are being organized around the country. Some of these are transitory and may not be effective over long periods of time. Basically they are group therapy organizations patterned after the principles of the successful Alcoholics Anonymous.

The Future

Drug abuse treatment can only succeed by correcting the basic problem of drug users, which is their inability to cope with the daily stresses of life. A compulsive drug user, addict, or alcoholic has relied for months or perhaps years on the external solace provided by drugs. A cure of this dependence requires him to redirect his attitudes toward his own weaknesses.

When the law is enforced, the drug abuser is taken out of his usual environment for a time. For the period of his jail sentence, an addict is "cured" simply because he is forced to do without drugs. A jail sentence protects society only temporarily from the harm that the drug user may do as he searches for drugs or while he is under their influence.

Abstinence from drugs is also enforced in private and public hospitals. Both addicted and nonaddicted drug abusers are withdrawn from drugs, given a period of recuperation and psychiatric therapy, and then released. But postinstitutional follow-up, which should be the most important part of any treatment program, is generally weak.

The complete cure of compulsive drug use is not at present a reliable prospect. The arresting of addiction, which would allow the individual to function within the bounds of society, may be the most practical outcome of treatment.

The rescue of a person from a possible life of compulsive drug abuse or alcoholism saves society a good deal more than the cost of his complete rehabilitation, maintenance on methadone, or maintenance within a therapeutic community. The more our nation's policymakers become convinced that the cost of ambitious, well-planned, humane programs is money well spent, the more progress in combatting drug abuse we can expect to witness.

The damage done to the individual and society is so powerful and so widespread that the only practical long-range cure is prevention through education.

Summary

I. Legal control of drugs

A. Early federal laws specified that opium, cocal leaves, marijuana, and peyote were "habit-forming narcotic drugs"
B. The Comprehensive Drug Abuse Prevention and Control Act (1970) completely redesigned older federal drug laws. Table 5.1 outlines the classes of drugs and the penalties for violations
C. State drug control laws

1. States are establishing laws similar to the federal Drug Abuse Prevention and Control Act

D. Juveniles and the law

1. Individuals under 18 to 21 years of age are usually subject to the same drug laws as adults
2. Proceedings regarding a crime are conducted in juvenile court

II. Legal control of drug abusers

A. Most drug control laws are directed toward the criminality of the individual, not his behavior
B. Enforcement of drug laws is means of control until research gives us knowledge to prevent drug abuse behavior

1. Some type of control is needed in any treatment program
2. More control than is necessary is actually punishment

C. Federal Narcotics Addict Rehabilitation Act of 1966 helps states and communities to treat drug abusers
D. Criminal commitment for drug abuse is a means for committing to a treatment program an individual convicted of a crime
E. Civil commitment for drug abuse is a legal mechanism used to ensure control over drug abusers during treatment and rehabilitation

III. Drug abuse therapy

A. Most drug users—experimenters and occasional users—given adequate supervision will eventually give up the illegal use of drugs

B. Medical authorities feel that the compulsive user, addict, or alcoholic is emotionally disturbed and often physically ill

1. These individuals need physical treatment and psychological help, often continuing throughout life
2. Most compulsive users would prefer not to stop using drugs, but return to controlled, moderate use
3. Return to controlled drug use is an unrealistic or impossible goal for most

C. Emergency therapy

1. In an emergency drug situation a physician needs to know certain information to treat a drug user
2. Often, after the initial emergency, little more than acceptance and reassurance is all that is necessary to relieve the anxiety and fear of a drug reaction

D. Use of drugs in the treatment of abuse

1. Treating drug abusers often involves the use of mood-modifying drugs

a. Methadone is often used in withdrawal from narcotics or solvents
b. Pentobarbital can be used in withdrawal from barbiturates or alcohol

2. Drug therapy for alcoholism

a. Tranquilizing drugs used to relieve anxiety, tremons, and the restlessness common to all drug abusers
b. Aversion therapy—use of drugs which make a person sick if he drinks beverages containing alcohol have been used for years

3. Maintenance treatment—giving the individual daily dosages of a substance which blocks the psychotropic effects of the drug he has been abusing
4. Narcotics antagonists—giving the individual drugs that can apparently occupy the place in the nervous system where narcotics act without producing the mood-modifying effects

E. Psychotherapy

1. Basis of all drug-abuse treatment programs
2. May be either a superficial emotional reinforcement or deep exploration of the subconscious mind

F. Therapeutic communities—complex social systems where an individual lives, works, and maintains all of his social contacts within the community
G. Alcoholics Anonymous—a loosely organized group of nondrinking alcoholics whose sole purpose is to help its members to stay sober

IV. The return to society

    A. The social pressures that led the addict to drug abuse are likely to be present when he returns to society

    B. Consequently, if he is returned to his community in gradual stages, or if he has not established a criminal record because of drug use, he has a much better chance of making an adjustment

    C. A felony conviction can also hamper the individual when he returns to society

    D. Programs are being developed to assist addicts in their attempts to return to their communities, and perhaps more important, to cope with drugs

V. The future

    A. Drug abuse treatment can only succeed by correcting the inadequate ability of individuals to combat the ordinary stresses of life

    B. A cure of dependence requires an individual to redirect his attitudes toward his own weaknesses

    C. The only practical long-range "cure" for drug abuse is prevention through education

VI. Abuse prevention programs: all programs recognize the fact that many young people are or will be involved with drugs—and they offer alternate decisions about the life without drugs

Questions for Review

1. One philosophy of drug abuse likens it to the infectious disease cycle. In this philosophy, what is the reservoir of infection; the infecting agents; the vectors? How can the cycle be stopped?

2. What underlying causes increased the use of drugs in the United States during the 1800s?

3. What does the term "dangerous drugs" mean? Are there restrictions on medical preparations of dangerous drugs?

4. Which states have led the way in the enactment of drug legislation in support of Federal laws? Are state laws uniform? Why?

5. What is the difference between methedrine and methadone? How are they used?

6. What problems does a narcotic addict face when he tries to return to a normal, drug-free life?

7. Several programs to assist drug users have emerged recently. What are they?

8. How would you help an ex-addict to return to society? Would you attempt to keep him away from all associations with drugs or drug users?

9. Which of the programs to help drug users do you think might be most effective? Why?

GLOSSARY

abstinence syndrome   Symptoms that result from withdrawal of alcohol, depressants, opiates, etc.

abuse   To use wrongly or improperly; misuse.

acute   Short duration.

addiction   The state of being given up to some habit, practice, or pursuit.

amphetamine   A central nervous system stimulant.

analgesic   A chemical or drug which has the ability to relieve pain.

anesthetic   Chemical, substance, or agent that produces insensibility to pain or touch.

barbital   (Diethylbarbituric acid) A long-duration sedative and hypnotic; a central nervous system depressant.

barbiturate   Drug used in medicine as a hypnotic or a sedative; a central nervous system depressant.

Benzedrine   A trade name for an amphetamine compound.

blackout   A period of temporary amnesia occurring while drinking.

caffeine   An alkaloid obtained from coffee, tea, etc. In medicine used as a stimulant.

carcinogen	Any chemical, substance, or agent that is capable of producing a cancer in the body.
cardiovascular	Pertaining to heart and blood vessels.
chronic	Something that continues for a long time.
cocaine	Drug used in medicine as a narcotic or local anesthetic; a central nervous system stimulant.
codeine	An analgesic, hypnotic, or sedative drug derived from opium.
coma	An abnormally deep stupor or sleep.
convulsions	Contortions of the body caused by violent muscular contractions.
delirium tremens	A psychic disorder involving hallucinations, both visual and auditory, delusions, incoherence, anxiety, and trembling; found in habitual users of alcoholic beverages and some drugs.
denature	To change the nature of a substance; to make it unfit for human consumption.
dependence	The psychophysical state of an addict or drug abuser.
depressant	A chemical, substance, or agent that has the ability to reduce the functional activity of the body.
depression	Reduction of the functional activity of the body.
Dexedrine	A trade name for an amphetamine.
distillation	The process of distilling and condensing vapor into a liquid.
dosage (dose)	Amount of a medicine to be taken at any one time.
epilepsy	A disturbance showing generalized convulsions.
ethyl acetate	Solvent used in the manufacture of plastic cements and glue.
euphoria	A feeling of well-being; in psychiatry, an abnormal or exaggerated sense of well-being.

habitual
: Tending to act in a certain way acquired by frequent repetitive actions or acts.

hallucination
: Perception of objects with no external reality.

hallucinogen
: A chemical, substance, or agent capable of producing hallucinations.

intoxication
: State of being poisoned; condition produced by excessive use (abuse) of a toxic drug, alcohol, barbiturates, etc.

intravenous
: Into a vein.

irritability
: The ability to respond to a stimulus.

isoamyl acetate
: Solvent used in the manufacture of plastic cements and glue.

lactose
: Milk sugar.

leucopenia
: Reduction of the number of white blood cells (leucocytes) in the blood.

marijuana
: Indian hemp (Cannabis sativa).

mescaline
: A poisonous oil extracted from peyote (Lophophora williamsii).

morphine
: A widely used analgesic and sedative d ug.

narcotic
: Having the power to produce a state of sleep or drowsiness.

nicotine
: A poisonous alkaloid that is the active product of tobacco.

opiate
: A drug containing or derived from opium; a narcotic.

opium
: A narcotic drug consisting of the dried juice of the opium poppy (Papaver somniferum).

paraldehyde
: A hypnotic drug derived from alcohol.

peyote
: A common name for the cactus Lophophora williamsii.

physiological
: Pertaining to the functioning of the body.

psychic
: Pertaining to the human mind or soul.

psychoactive	Capable of altering psychic states such as mood, perception, and consciousness.
psychogenic	Originating in the mind.
psychological	Pertaining to the mind.
psychosis	A major mental disorder in which there is a departure from normal thinking, feeling, and acting. Loss of contact with reality.
psychotherapy	The science or art of curing psychological abnormalities or disorders.
psychotogenic	Psychosis-producing.
psychotomimetic	Psychosis-mimicking.
sedative	A medicine used to depress excitement.
stimulant	Any chemical, substance, or agent that temporarily increases the activity of the body or nervous system.
subcutaneous	Under the skin.
synthetic	Formed by a chemical reaction in a laboratory.
thrombocytopenia	Reduction of the number of platelets in the blood.
tolerance	Increasing resistance to the usual effects of a drug.
toxicity	The quality of being poisonous.
tranquilizer	A drug that acts on the emotional state of overactive and disturbed individuals.

BIBLIOGRAPHY

Bergersen, Betty S. and Krug, Elsie E., *Pharmacology in Nursing,* 11th. ed., St. Louis: Mosby, 1971.

Birdwood, George, *Willing Victim: A Parent's Guide to Drug Abuse,* New York: International Publishers, 1970.

Chayet, Neil, "Old Laws for New Junkies," *Emergency Medicine,* No. 4, April, 1971: pp. 216, 217, 221.

Ewing, John A., "Students, Sex, and Marihuana," *Medical Aspects of Human Sexuality,* Vol. 6, No. 2, February, 1972: pp. 102–103.

"Exploring the Nature of Heroin Addiction," *Medical World News,* Vol. 12, No. 33, September 10, 1971: pp. 57–63, 66.

The Health Consequences of Smoking, U.S. Public Health Service Publication No. 1696, Washington, D.C., U.S. Government Printing Office, 1968.

Hollister, Leo E., "Current Research on Marijuana," *The Journal of Social Issues,* Vol. 27, No. 3, 1971: pp. 23–33.

Jellinek, E. M., *The Disease Concept of Alcoholism,* Highland Park, N.J.: Hill-House Press, 1960.

Jellinek, E. M., "Phases of Alcohol Addiction," *Quarterly Journal of Studies on Alcohol,* Vol. 13, 1952: pp. 673–678.

Non-Medical Use of Drugs: Interim Report of the Canadian Government's Commission of Inquiry, New York: Penguin, 1971.

Nowlis, Helen, *Drugs on the College Campus,* Garden City, N.Y.: McGraw-Hill, 1969.

Paton, W. D. M. and Crown, June (eds.), *Cannabis and Its Derivatives: Pharmacology and Applied Psychology,* London, England: Oxford University Press, 1972.

Peterson, Robert C., "Marihuana and Health—The American Cannabis Research Program," *Mental Health Digest,* Vol. 3, No. 12, December, 1971: pp.13–20.

Snyder, S. H., *Uses of Marijuana,* New York: Oxford University Press, 1971.

Terry, Luther L. (chairman), *11, 12, 13, World Conference on Smoking and Health,* National Interagency Council on Smoking and Health, New York: 1967.

Zwerding, D., "Methaqualone: The Safe Drug That Isn't Very," *The Washington Post,* November 12, 1972: p. B-3.

INDEX

Italic numbers refer to pages with tables or illustrations.

Printer and Binder: Halliday Lithograph

78 79 80 9 8 7 6 5 4 3